COOKING

WITH WILD BERRIES & FRUITS

OF MINNESOTA, WISCONSIN AND MICHIGAN

T0166307

by Teresa Marrone

Adventure Publications, Inc.
Cambridge, MN

ACKNOWLEDGMENTS

Thanks to Michelle Hueser of *Edible Twin Cities* for her review of the book.

Cover and book design by Jonathan Norberg

Cover photos: black raspberries, blueberries, grapes, ground cherries, red chokecherries and serviceberries by Teresa Marrone

Edited by Brett Ortler

10 9 8 7 6 5 4 3 2

TABLE OF CONTENTS

Introduction 4

Autumn Olive 6

Blackberries and
Black Dewberries.....................................11

Blueberries, Bilberries and
Huckleberries 18

Bunchberries.. 30

Pin Cherry, Black Cherry,
Chokecherry and Sand Cherry 31

Chokeberries or Aronia 38

Crabapples 42

Cranberries...47

Creeping Oregon Grape......................... 53

Currants.. 54

Elderberries 62

Gooseberries.. 68

Grapes...76

Ground Cherries 78

Hackberries 84

Hawthorns 86

Highbush Cranberries 89

Juniper.. 97

Mountain Ash... 98

Mulberries 102

Nannyberries, Withe-Rod and
Blackhaws... 108

American Wild Plum............................. 112

Red Raspberries, Black Raspberries and
Dewberries..118

Rose Hips..126

Russian Olives 130

Serviceberries 133

Northern Spicebush............................. 140

Strawberries...142

Sumac: Smooth, Staghorn and
Fragrant 148

Thimbleberries 152

Wintergreen and
Creeping Snowberry..............................155

Mixed Berry Dishes 156

Six Recipes Using Wild Fruit
Juice or Syrup 158

General Instructions and
Information... 163

Index...172

INTRODUCTION

Wild berries and fruits are everywhere, once you learn to look for them. You'll find raspberries growing in the shrubby areas around the playground, elderberries on the edges of cattail swamps, and nannyberries growing in forest remnants that have been kept as buffers around office parks. Some species, like blueberries, blackberries and raspberries, look just like commercially available fruits, although in the wild they are usually smaller. Others have never been commercialized, and so will be unfamiliar at first.

This book celebrates edible wild berries and fruits. It includes information and recipes for over 40 species that are found in our area. (For more information on identifying these plants, please see the companion book, *Wild Berries & Fruits Field Guide of Minnesota, Wisconsin and Michigan*). Here you'll find recipes for sauces, baked goods, and other foods made with these delicious wild fruits.

One thing to keep in mind is that wild fruits are much less consistent than domestic fruits, which have been bred for specific flavor characteristics (as well as the ability to withstand the rigors of packing and shipping). When working with wild fruits, it may be necessary to adjust the amount of sugar, for example, if the fruit you've picked isn't as sweet as it might be. If you use wild fruits in recipes calling for the same type of domestic fruit, you may need to adjust quantities; wild fruits are typically smaller and pack more closely together, so a cup of wild blueberries weighs more than a cup of domestic blueberries.

Another very important thing to remember is that wild fruits have not been thoroughly tested for possible adverse reactions in sensitive individuals. Some foods—both wild and domestic—simply don't agree with everyone. When you're sampling a wild fruit for the first time, eat only a small portion to make sure that you won't have a problem.

It is also worth stressing that before eating something which you've harvested from the wild, you must be *absolutely certain* that the plant has been identified properly. Further, it's important to realize that even if the fruit of a plant is edible, the leaves and other parts may make you sick if you eat them. Some fruits are mildly toxic when under-ripe; others have pits or seeds that contain harmful substances, and so require specific preparation. This book attempts to alert the reader to possible problems, but it's still a good practice to get assistance from a knowledgeable forager before harvesting or preparing unfamiliar wild foods.

How This Book Is Organized

Fruits are listed in alphabetical order, by their common name. In several cases, similar fruits have been grouped because they are interchangeable in recipes; for example, blueberries, huckleberries and bilberries are in one section.

Each species includes a bit of general information about the plant, including any harvesting tips that might be particularly helpful. If the fruit is commonly juiced, instructions are included with this general information. You'll learn how to successfully preserve your harvest by freezing, if appropriate. Recipes for each species are included; and at the end of each species, there's a list of recipes elsewhere in the book that use that particular fruit, as well as some quick ideas for using the fruit.

After the individual species, there are several recipes that use mixed fruits, as well as six recipes using juice or syrup from virtually any of the fruits in this book. Following this are instructions on how to make jelly and jam; each species includes measurements for making jelly and jam (when appropriate), but rather than repeating the same instructions multiple times, the specific instructions are written on pgs. 164–167. The book concludes with general information that pertains to many different fruits, such as instructions on dehydrating berries and fruits, making fruit leather, and instructions for sterilizing jars and canning.

You'll also find useful tips throughout the book. These explain things like how to make a lattice-top pie crust, zesting lemons and other citrus fruits, and how to make an improvised double boiler. These tips apply to a number of recipes in the book and will make cooking easier.

AUTUMN OLIVE *(Elaeagnus umbellata)*

Here's a fruit that definitely doesn't look—or cook—like anything you can buy in the store. Ripe fruits are soft and red, and covered with silvery scales; they look like they've been rolled in a subtle glitter. Fruits are borne profusely on the shrubs, so it's easy to gather a good quantity; a step ladder will help you reach fruits near the top of the shrub. Choose fruits that are soft and red; unripe fruits aren't sweet.

Autumn olive fruits have a large, inedible pit. It can be removed by cooking the fruits, then straining or puréeing the mixture. For purée with a fresher taste, some cooks prefer to process the fruits through a food mill without cooking first; they're juicy enough that they don't need cooking to soften them first (although the yield will be slightly higher if the fruit is cooked because the added water helps separate the flesh from the pits). I've also heard that a juicer works well on autumn olives, to prepare fresh (uncooked) juice; I've never tried this, but if you have a juicer, give it a go.

Some amateur winemakers use autumn olive fruit to make a light red wine. An Internet search for "autumn olive wine" will provide a number of recipes to try.

When I'm making purée, I remove the stemlets before any processing, whether I'm cooking the fruits or not. Some don't bother, but I don't like small bits of stem in my finished purée, and feel it is worth the time. It works best to pinch the stem off with your fingernails rather than pulling it off; the soft fruit may split from the pressure of pulling.

To make uncooked autumn olive purée, place fruits (preferably with the stems removed) in a food mill set over a large bowl; it's easiest to work with no more than 2 cups at a time. Turn the paddle until the fruits are smashed and as much pulp as possible has passed through the screen into the bowl. The large pits prevent all of the pulp from going through because the pulp is trapped around the pits and the paddle can't reach it. Now use a stiff rubber spatula to press the softened pulp through the holes; the spatula is much better for working around the hard pits. Processed in this fashion, a quart of ripe fruit will yield about 1 cup of thick, rich red purée that resembles tomato paste.

To prepare juice or cooked purée, measure the fruit and place in a non-aluminum pot; for juice, it's not necessary to remove the stemlets but for purée, it's preferable to remove them as described above. For juice, add 3 cups water per quart of fruit; for purée, add 1 cup water per quart of fruit. Heat to boiling, then reduce the heat; cover and simmer for about 10 minutes, gently crushing the fruit with a potato masher near the end of cooking. **For juice,** transfer the mixture to a strainer lined with doubled, dampened cheesecloth and let it drip for 30 minutes; if you're making jelly, don't squeeze the fruit or the jelly will be cloudy. After the clear liquid has dripped away, set it aside and squeeze the fruit into a different container; you can use this slightly cloudy juice as a beverage or for cooking. **For purée,** process the cooked fruit through a food mill, pressing with a rubber spatula as noted above. Processed this way, a quart of fruit will yield about 3½ cups of lovely red juice, or about 1½ cups of purée that is thinner than the purée from uncooked fruit.

Sweet Autumn Olive Bread

This bread has a sweet surprise in the center: a layer of brown sugar and nuts. Prepared buttermilk baking mix makes it quick and easy to prepare.

⅓ cup (packed) brown sugar

½ cup chopped walnuts, hickory nuts or other nuts

¼ teaspoon nutmeg

3 eggs

3 tablespoons vegetable oil

3 tablespoons cream

¾ cup autumn olive purée from cooked fruits (see note below)

⅔ cup white sugar

2¼ cups buttermilk baking mix

Heat oven to 350°F. Spray a standard-sized loaf pan generously with nonstick spray; set aside. In small bowl, combine brown sugar, nuts and nutmeg, mixing well with your fingers or a fork; set aside.

Add eggs, oil and cream to a mixing bowl; beat well with fork. Add autumn olive purée and white sugar, and beat together. Add baking mix, and stir with the fork until mix is completely moistened; there may still be a few small lumps in the batter.

Pour half of the batter into the prepared loaf pan, spreading evenly. Sprinkle brown sugar mixture evenly over batter; top with remaining batter. Bake for 50 to 60 minutes, or until toothpick inserted in center comes out clean. Remove from oven and let stand 10 minutes. Run a table knife around the edges to loosen, then turn out onto plate. Let cool for at least 1 hour before slicing.

If you've made your autumn olive purée from uncooked fruits, it will be a bit thicker than it should be for this recipe. Use a bit less than ¾ cup of the thicker purée, and add a little water to thin it a bit.

Autumn Olive "Berries" for Baking

About ¼ cup "berries" per ½ cup purée

Autumn olives can't be used whole for baking or recipes, as you could use, say, blueberries. The large, hard pits need to be removed first, and by the time that's done, what's left is just a small pile of wet skin with a little pulp. Here's a way to turn fruit purée into raisin-like morsels, which can be used in muffins or quick breads.

The "berries" are prepared from purée that is shaped, then dried in a dehydrator or your oven. Before starting, please read the section on dehydrating berries and fruits (pg. 168). Purée made from uncooked autumn olive fruits is thick enough to make the berries with no cooking. But if your purée was made with cooked fruits, or if you're substituting thinner purée from a different fruit, you'll have to cook the purée in a saucepan until it thickens before making the berries. It needs to be almost as thick as tomato paste, and there should be no liquid oozing around the bottom when you stir the purée.

Start with only one-third of the purée you want to use. Drop the purée in small rounded mounds, about the size of a canned kidney bean, onto a liner sheet if using a dehydrator, or onto a baking sheet lined with plastic wrap if using the oven. Keep ½ inch between the drops so they don't run together. Dry at 145°-150°F for 2 hours; keep remaining purée in the refrigerator during this time.

After 2 hours, use half of the remaining purée to spoon another kidney-bean-sized mound onto the drops that you've been drying. Dry for another 2 or 3 hours, or until the drops are solid enough to flip over (use a table knife if necessary to scrape the drops off the liner, then flip them). Spoon remaining purée on top of the flipped drops. Dry until firm and no longer sticky, typically another 3 to 5 hours; total drying time is 7 to 10 hours, but this varies depending on how wet the purée was. When berries are completely dry, transfer to a glass jar. Store in a cool place, checking several times in the first week to make sure they aren't emitting any moisture; if there is any moisture in the jar, return berries to dehydrator and dry some more. For storage longer than a few weeks, store in freezer.

Substitutions: You may substitute thick purée from highbush cranberries, crabapples, nannyberries or other fruits (cooked to thicken if necessary, as described above) for the autumn olive purée.

 These "berries" don't hold up in pie, sauce or other long-simmered dishes; they turn back into purée.

Refrigerator Cookies with Autumn Olive "Berries"

About 24 cookies

The nutmeg and brandy add a delightfully different taste to these crisp, buttery cookies. Make a batch of the dough in the morning and pop it in the refrigerator. Later in the day, it'll be easy to slice off and have fresh-baked cookies for an after-school snack.

½ cup (1 stick) unsalted butter, softened

¾ cup sugar

1 egg

1 tablespoon brandy or cognac, or ¼ teaspoon brandy extract

½ teaspoon nutmeg

1¾ cups all-purpose flour

⅓ to ½ cup dried autumn olive "berries"

In mixing bowl, cream butter with electric mixer until light and fluffy. Add sugar; beat until fluffy. Add egg and beat well. Add brandy and nutmeg; beat until smooth. In another mixing bowl, combine flour and dried berries; stir to blend. Add flour mixture to butter mixture; stir with a wooden spoon until soft dough forms (do not overmix, or the cookies will be tough). Transfer dough to a 1-gallon zipper-style food storage bag. Using your hands to press the dough together from the outside, form it into a firmly packed cylinder at the bottom of the bag, rolling it on the counter to smooth the shape; it will be about 2 inches around. Seal the bag and refrigerate for at least 5 hours, or overnight.

When you're ready to bake, heat oven to 350°F. Line 2 baking sheets with kitchen parchment, or spray with nonstick spray. Slit the plastic bag open to expose the roll of dough. Use a very sharp knife to cut the roll into ¼-inch-thick slices; transfer to prepared baking sheets. Bake for 10 minutes, then rotate pans (see "Rotating Cookies while Baking," below). Continue baking until lightly browned around the edges, 9 to 13 minutes longer. Transfer to wire rack to cool.

Variation: Refrigerator Cookies with Dried Berries
Follow recipe above, substituting dried blueberries, raspberries, serviceberries or strawberries for the autumn olive "berries."

Rotating Cookies while Baking
If you're baking more than one sheet of cookies, they tend to bake unevenly because the pan on top blocks heat to the pan (or pans) below it. To help ensure even cooking, rotate the pans about halfway through baking, moving the top pan to the lower shelf and moving the lower pan to the top shelf; as you do this, also rotate the pans so the edge that was at the front of the oven is now in the back of the oven.

Autumn Olive Jelly

3 cups autumn olive juice

1 tablespoon lemon juice

Half of a 1.75-ounce box powdered pectin

½ teaspoon butter, optional (helps reduce foaming)

3¼ cups sugar

Prepare and process as directed in Jelly Instructions (using pectin), pg. 164.

Autumn Olive Jam

2 cups autumn olive purée

Half of a 1.75-ounce box powdered pectin

2 tablespoons lemon juice

2¾ cups sugar

Prepare and process as directed in Jam Instructions (using pectin), pg. 167.

Other recipes in this book featuring autumn olives:

Six Recipes Using Wild Fruit Juice or Syrup, pgs. 158–162
Wild Berry or Fruit Syrup, pg. 163
Wild Berry or Fruit Leather, pg. 170
As a variation in Cookies with Dried Fruit, Nuts and White Chocolate Chips,
pg. 28

BLACKBERRIES and BLACK DEWBERRIES
(Blackberries, Rubus allegheniensis; dewberries, R. hispidus and others)

The common blackberry (*Rubus allegheniensis*) is the wild version of the familiar fruit found in the supermarket; like many wild fruits, it is smaller than its domestic counterparts. Bristly dewberries are one of numerous species of dewberries that are black when ripe; all can be used in the same way. (To avoid cumbersome ingredients lists, the recipes on the following pages all call for blackberries, but you can use black dewberries instead—or even a mix of two fruits.)

Besides color, another thing that these fruits have in common are seeds ... lots and lots of them. They're harder than seeds found in raspberries, and can make jam or desserts seem almost crunchy. Some people prefer to strain cooked or crushed blackberries to remove the seeds. For most dishes, I like the texture that the whole or lightly crushed fruits provide. (See pg. 17 for a jam recipe that is a compromise; half of the seeds are strained out, while the rest of the fruit provides texture to the jam.)

Blackberries and bristly dewberries ripen late in the season, when many other berries are finished. They seem to pick up extra taste over their slow ripening; although a bit less sweet than many other berries, they have a deeper, more interesting flavor.

To prepare purée or juice, measure the fruit and place in a non-aluminum pot. For purée, add ½ cup water per quart of fruit; for juice, add 1 cup water per quart of fruit. Gently crush the fruit with a potato masher to start the juices flowing. Heat to boiling, then reduce the heat; cover and simmer for about 10 minutes. **For seedless purée,** process the cooked fruit through a food mill, then discard the seeds; if you don't mind the seeds, the purée is ready after cooking. **For juice,** transfer the mixture to a strainer lined with doubled, dampened cheesecloth and let it drip for 30 minutes; if you're making jelly, don't squeeze the fruit or the jelly will be cloudy. After the clear liquid has dripped away, set it aside and squeeze the fruit into a different container; you can use this slightly cloudy juice as a beverage or for cooking. Processed this way, a quart of fruit will yield about 1½ cups of purée, or about 2 cups of juice.

Blackberries can be frozen for later use in jam, pies and other cooked desserts. Simply lay them on a baking sheet in a single layer and freeze; when the berries are solid, pack them into plastic bags or freezer containers for storage.

Blackberry Turnovers

4 turnovers

Wild blackberries are much smaller than domestic blackberries, and tuck nicely into these individual turnovers.

1½ cups fresh blackberries (about 7 ounces)

⅓ cup shredded Granny Smith apple (about one-quarter of an apple)

3 tablespoons sugar, plus additional for sprinkling on crust

1 tablespoon all-purpose flour, plus additional for rolling out pastry

Ready-to-use pastry for single-crust pie

A little cream for brushing turnovers

Heat oven to 375°F. In mixing bowl, combine blackberries, shredded apple, 3 tablespoons sugar and 1 tablespoon flour. Stir gently to mix; set aside for 10 minutes.

While fruit is standing, prepare crusts: Divide pastry into 4 equal portions. On a lightly floured worksurface, roll each into a circle about 6 inches across. Divide fruit mixture evenly between circles, mounding in center. Brush edges lightly with water. Fold each circle in half; seal edges well with a fork. Place on baking sheet. Brush tops lightly with cream; sprinkle with sugar. Make several small slits in the top of each turnover. Bake until crust is golden brown and the filling is bubbling in the slits, 25 to 30 minutes.

Smooth Blackberry Sauce

About 1 cup

This type of sauce is sometimes called a coulis. *It's excellent when used to top ice cream, French toast or cooked cereal. For an elegant dessert, spoon a puddle of the sauce onto individual dessert plates, then top with a piece of cheesecake or a poached pear.*

1 cup strained, seedless blackberry purée

¼ to ½ cup sugar

**⅛ teaspoon grated lemon zest
(colored rind only, with none of the white pith)**

In small, heavy-bottomed non-aluminum saucepan, combine purée, ¼ cup sugar, and the lemon zest. Heat over medium-high heat, stirring constantly, until boiling. Cook, stirring constantly, until purée has thickened to a sauce-like consistency. Taste, and add additional sugar if needed; if you do add more sugar, cook the sauce for another few minutes, stirring constantly, to dissolve the sugar. Cool before using.

Wild Berry Vinegar
1 quart

Use in salad dressings, or in marinades for poultry, meat or fish. This makes a lovely gift.

1 pint blackberries, raspberries, strawberries, elderberries or highbush cranberries

1 quart white wine vinegar

You'll need a glass bottle that holds at least 2 quarts for this, with a mouth wide enough to insert the berries; juice is often sold in these types of bottles. Wash it very well, then fill it with boiling water and let stand for at least 5 minutes.

Drain water from bottle; add berries. In medium saucepan, heat vinegar over low heat until it just begins to steam; don't let vinegar boil. Pour warm vinegar over berries in bottle. Let stand until cooled to room temperature, then seal bottle and shake gently. Set bottle in dark, cool place for 1 week, shaking occasionally. Strain through a sieve lined with a paper coffee filter into clean 1-quart measuring cup with a spout; discard berries. Pour vinegar into a clean bottle. It will keep, at room temperature, for at least 6 months.

 For a more decorative presentation, spear a few fresh berries and a curl of lemon zest on a wooden skewer; place skewer in the storage bottle before adding strained, finished vinegar to the bottle. (Be sure to wash the lemon well before making the zest curl.)

Blackberry Sidecar
Per serving

This is a strong drink, so try it when you don't have anywhere to drive!

2 ounces gin

1 ounce triple sec liqueur

1 tablespoon blackberry syrup (pg. 163)

1 tablespoon lime juice

2 or 3 fresh blackberries for garnish, optional

Combine gin, triple sec, blackberry syrup and lime juice in a shaker filled with crushed ice. Cover and shake well. Strain into a chilled cocktail glass; garnish with fresh blackberries. Call a cab.

Blackberry Filling

About ½ cup; easily increased

This filling is dark, thick, glossy and totally luscious.

½ teaspoon water

½ teaspoon cornstarch

6 ounces fresh or previously frozen blackberries (about 1¼ cups)

1 tablespoon grated apple

1½ tablespoons sugar

In small bowl, blend together water and cornstarch; set aside. In small, heavy-bottomed non-aluminum saucepan, combine blackberries, apple and sugar. Crush fruit gently with a potato masher to start juices flowing. Heat to boiling over medium-high heat, then cook, stirring frequently, until mixture is no longer runny; this will take 9 to 11 minutes. Add cornstarch mixture, stirring constantly; cook for about 1 minute longer, or until thick. Cool completely before using.

Use this to prepare Easy Bear Claws (pg. 20), Fruit-Striped Cookie Fingers (pg. 119), or Fruit-Filled Muffins (pg. 146). Refrigerate extra filling, and use to top oatmeal or toast.

Blackberry Jelly

4 half-pints

2¾ cups blackberry juice

2 tablespoons lemon juice

Two-thirds of a 1.75-ounce box powdered pectin

½ teaspoon butter, optional (helps reduce foaming)

3½ cups sugar

Prepare and process as directed in Jelly Instructions (using pectin), pg. 164.

Blackberry-Apple Crisp

The combination of blackberries and apples makes a wonderful crisp—the color is lovely, and the mix of tart and sweet is just right. Serve with a scoop of vanilla ice cream.

2 large cooking apples such as Granny Smith, Fireside or McIntosh

2 cups fresh or previously frozen blackberries (about 10 ounces)

2 teaspoons cornstarch

½ cup all-purpose flour

½ cup (packed) golden brown sugar

½ teaspoon cinnamon

¼ teaspoon nutmeg

4 tablespoons (half of a stick) cold butter, cut into pieces

¼ cup quick-cooking rolled oats

Heat oven to 375°F. Spray 8-inch-square baking dish with nonstick spray. Peel and core apples, then chop them coarsely in food processor or by hand; place in prepared dish. Add blackberries and cornstarch; stir gently to mix. Set aside.

In mixing bowl, combine flour, brown sugar, cinnamon and nutmeg; stir to mix. Add butter; blend with your fingertips (or a fork) until the mixture is the texture of very coarse sand, with a few pea-sized pieces of butter remaining. Stir in rolled oats. Sprinkle the mixture evenly over the fruit. Bake until topping is golden-brown and filling bubbles, 35 to 45 minutes. Let cool on wire rack at least 15 minutes before serving; serve warm or at room temperature.

Substitutions: Blueberries, serviceberries or raspberries may be substituted for the blackberries in this simple crisp.

 *When making the topping for a crisp, don't over-mix or make it too fine. It's easiest to sprinkle when it's still got some coarse bits in it, and it comes out with a better texture than if it is well blended.*

Blackberry Freezer Jam

4 half-pints

The fruit is not cooked when preparing this easy jam; it has a fresh, vibrant flavor.

1 quart blackberries

1³/₄ cups sugar

Two-thirds of a 1.75-ounce box powdered pectin
(see pg. 164 for information on dividing pectin)

²/₃ cup water

Prepare 4 half-pint canning jars, bands and lids as described on pg. 171, or have clean plastic freezer containers ready (see tip below). Crush fruit with a potato masher in a mixing bowl, or chop to medium consistency in food processor (don't overprocess; jam should have small fruit chunks in it). Measure 1¾ cups crushed or chopped fruit; use any leftover fruit to top ice cream or cook in other recipes. Place measured fruit and the sugar in a large ceramic or Pyrex mixing bowl. Stir well; set aside for 10 minutes, stirring several times with a wooden spoon.

When fruit has rested for 10 minutes, prepare pectin. In small non-aluminum saucepan, combine pectin and water; stir well (mixture may be lumpy). Heat to a full, rolling boil over high heat, stirring constantly. Cook at a rolling boil for 1 minute, stirring constantly. Pour pectin mixture into fruit in bowl. Stir constantly with a wooden spoon until sugar is completely dissolved and no longer grainy, about 3 minutes; a few grains may remain, but the mixture should no longer look cloudy (or the jam will be cloudy).

Pour into prepared jars or containers, leaving ½ inch headspace; cover with clean lids. Let stand at room temperature for 24 hours; the jam should set (it may be softer than regular jam, especially at first; that's okay). If jam is not set, refrigerate for several days until set before using or freezing. Use within 3 weeks, or freeze until needed; thaw frozen jam in refrigerator.

 Special plastic containers, designed especially for freezing, are available with the canning supplies at the supermarket.

Smoother Blackberry Jam

Blackberry jam has a wonderful, deep flavor, but some find it too seedy to enjoy. This recipe removes about half of the seeds; this leaves enough whole berries for a good texture.

5 cups fresh blackberries

2 tablespoons lemon juice

Half of a 1.75-ounce package powdered pectin

3¼ cups sugar

Place blackberries in mixing bowl; crush with potato masher. Transfer half of the crushed berries to a wire-mesh strainer set over another mixing bowl; press through with wooden spoon to strain seeds. Measure strained blackberries; add crushed blackberries to equal 2½ cups. Transfer measured fruit to 3-quart (or larger) heavy-bottomed non-aluminum pot (reserve any remaining fruit to top ice cream). Prepare and process as directed in Jam Instructions (using pectin), pg. 167.

Other recipes in this book featuring blackberries or dewberries:
>Rice Pudding with Wild Berries, pg. 107
>Fruits of the Forest Pie, pg. 156
>Brambleberry Cream Sauce, pg. 157
>Six Recipes Using Wild Fruit Juice or Syrup, pgs. 158–162
>Wild Berry or Fruit Syrup, pg. 163
>As a variation in Mulberry Ripple Cheesecake, pg. 104
>As a variation in Thimbleberry Smoothie, pg. 152
>As a substitute in Sautéed Fish with Thimbleberries, pg. 153

Quick ideas for using blackberries or dewberries:
>When making apple pie, reduce the amount of apples by 1 cup and add a cup of fresh or previously frozen blackberries or dewberries.

BLUEBERRIES, BILBERRIES and HUCKLEBERRIES

(Blueberries, *Vaccinium* spp.; bilberries, *V. cespitosum and others*; huckleberries, *Gaylussacia baccata*)

Other than raspberries (pg. 118), blueberries are probably the wild fruit that is picked most often. They are widespread in our region, and the wild fruits look just like a small version of the familiar domestic fruits; they're delicious raw or cooked. Bilberries and huckleberries are much less familiar, but equally delicious, and can be used in the same way as blueberries. You may also encounter the less-common mountain fly honeysuckle (*Lonicera villosa*), a shrub with oblong blue berries; they are a bit bitter, but can be used in blueberry recipes.

Blueberries are one of the first plants to grow in an area that has been swept by forest fire; I've been stunned to see literal fields of blue in rocky areas near Minnesota's Boundary Waters Canoe Area that had burned the previous year.

Wild blueberries have much more flavor than domestic blueberries, probably because they are smaller and have more of the flavorful skin in proportion to the flesh. If you're substituting wild blueberries in a recipe that was written for domestic blueberries, you should use a bit less by volume than called for; the smaller wild blueberries pack more closely in the measuring cup, so a cup of wild blueberries weighs more than a cup of domestic blueberries. Huckleberries are similar in size to wild blueberries, and a bit less juicy; bilberries are a bit smaller. (To avoid cumbersome ingredients lists, the recipes that follow all call for blueberries, but you can use bilberries or huckleberries instead—or a mix of fruits.)

It's easy to gather a decent quantity of wild blueberries, once you've found a good patch; huckleberries and bilberries tend to be more scattered, so you might end up mixing them with your wild blueberry haul to get a sufficient quantity for use in recipes. They often grow in the same areas, so if you find huckleberries or bilberries, chances are good that you'll be adding blueberries to the bucket at the same time. If you can travel to an area that had a forest fire the previous year, you should enjoy phenomenal berry picking.

Blueberries, bilberries and huckleberries are rich in anthocyanins, antioxidants believed to have numerous health benefits. All three fruits can be eaten raw or cooked. Huckleberries have crunchy seeds, so some cooks prefer to strain them out when using them in cooked dishes; seeds of blueberries and bilberries are soft and unnoticeable. The berries store well in the refrigerator, remaining fresh for up to a week; don't wash them until you're ready to use them, though, or they may mold.

They're easy to freeze; simply wash and pat dry, then spread in a single layer on a baking sheet and freeze overnight. The next day, transfer the individually frozen berries to freezer containers, and freeze for up to 6 months. Finally, all three berries can be successfully dried in a dehydrator, and used in trail mixes and an out-of-hand snack, or to substitute for raisins or craisins in recipes. Most people prefer to use these berries whole, but they can be juiced; the juice is an excellent beverage, sweetened as needed, and can also be used to make jelly. To prepare juice, follow the instructions for making blackberry juice on pg. 11; to make jelly, follow the proportions for autumn olive jelly on pg. 10.

Classic Blueberry Pie

Wild blueberries give this traditional pie an exceptional flavor.

1 quart fresh or previously frozen blueberries

1 cup sugar

¼ cup quick-cooking tapioca

1 tablespoon lemon juice

½ teaspoon cinnamon

½ teaspoon nutmeg

Pinch of salt

Ready-to-use pastry for double-crust pie

2 tablespoons butter, cut into pieces

1 egg, lightly beaten

Heat oven to 375°F. In mixing bowl, combine blueberries, sugar, tapioca, lemon juice, cinnamon, nutmeg and salt. Stir gently until well-mixed; set aside for 15 minutes.

Fit one pastry into ungreased deep-dish pie plate. Scrape blueberry mixture into pie plate. Scatter butter pieces over blueberries. Moisten edges of pastry in pie plate with a little cold water, then top with second pastry. Seal, trim and flute edges. Cut 6 to 8 inch-long slits in the crust. Place pie on baking sheet (to catch drips). Brush top with beaten egg. Bake until crust is golden and filling bubbles through slits, 35 to 40 minutes. Transfer to rack to cool; best served warm.

 For extra sparkle and flavor, sprinkle a tablespoon of sugar over the top crust after brushing it with the egg.

Easy Bear Claws

8 rolls

This quick version of a bakery staple uses refrigerated biscuits to eliminate complicated pastry-making. Quick, easy—and delicious.

1 tube (8 biscuits; 16.3 ounces) refrigerated "grand-sized" flaky biscuits (reduced-fat works fine)

All-purpose flour for rolling dough

½ cup Blueberry Filling (pg. 23), or other wild fruit filling (see "Filling options" below)

1 egg, beaten with 1 teaspoon water

¼ cup sliced almonds

2 tablespoons coarse sugar such as turbinado

Heat oven to 375°F. Line 2 rimmed baking sheets with kitchen parchment; set aside.

Separate dough into 8 biscuits. On lightly floured worksurface, gently roll one to an oval that is 4 inches across and about 6 inches long. Spoon one-eighth of the filling mixture onto the center of the dough. Fold the dough over to make a half-moon. Press edges together very well, lifting the edge and pinching all around with your fingertips. Place on a prepared baking sheet. Repeat with remaining dough and filling, keeping at least 1 inch between the rolls.

With a very sharp knife, make 4 cuts through the sealed edge, cutting about halfway into the crescent. Fan the cut strips out slightly to resemble a bear's paw. Brush dough with beaten egg; sprinkle with almonds and sugar. Bake for 8 minutes, then switch the baking sheets so the one underneath moves to the top shelf. Continue baking until golden brown and cooked through, 9 to 12 minutes longer; when the rolls are properly cooked, the dough should not feel mushy when pressed gently with a fingertip. Remove from oven and let stand about a minute, then transfer rolls to wire rack to cool for at least 15 minutes before serving. Best served warm, the day they are made.

Filling options: This recipe works with any of the following fillings: Blackberry (pg. 14), Blueberry (pg. 23), Crabapple (pg. 45), Green Gooseberry (pg. 71), Ground Cherry (pg. 82), Mulberry (pg. 105), Nannyberry (pg. 111), Plum (pg. 117), Raspberry (pg. 121), Serviceberry (pg. 136), Strawberry (pg. 145), or Thimbleberry (pg. 154).

 Be sure to buy the extra-large biscuits; standard-sized biscuits won't work here.

Blueberry Streusel Muffins

A tasty streusel topping adds interest to these delicious muffins.

Streusel

⅓ **cup sugar**

¼ **cup all-purpose flour**

½ **teaspoon cinnamon**

4 tablespoons (half of a stick) cold butter, cut into pieces

½ **cup sugar**

½ **cup (1 stick) butter, softened**

1 egg

1 teaspoon vanilla extract

2¼ **cups all-purpose flour**

1 tablespoon plus 1 teaspoon baking powder

¼ **teaspoon salt**

1 cup whole milk, divided

1 to 1¼ cups fresh or still-frozen blueberries (4½ to 5½ ounces)

Heat oven to 375°F. Line 12-cup muffin tin with paper liners; set aside. Make the streusel: In a small bowl, stir together the sugar, flour and cinnamon. Add butter; use a fork or your fingertips to blend the butter into the sugar mixture, working them together until mixture is the texture of very coarse sand with some pea-sized particles. Set aside.

In mixing bowl, beat sugar and butter with an electric mixer until fluffy. Add egg and vanilla; beat well. Place a wire-mesh strainer over a plate; add flour, baking powder and salt. Shake the strainer over the mixing bowl until half of the flour has been added to the butter mixture. Stir with a wooden spoon until just moistened. Add half of the milk; stir until combined. Add remaining flour and milk in the same manner. Add blueberries and stir very gently until incorporated. Spoon batter into prepared muffin cups. Spoon streusel over batter. Bake until golden brown and springy to the touch, 25 to 30 minutes.

Substitution: Use 1¼ cups serviceberries in place of the blueberries.

If you're using frozen blueberries, don't thaw them before mixing into the batter; add them while still frozen. This prevents soggy, purple muffins.

Blueberry Jalousie (Window-Blind Tart)　　6 servings

Frozen puff pastry makes this fancy-looking dessert easy to make; the instructions look complicated, but it's a snap to prepare.

1½ cups fresh or previously frozen blueberries (about 7 ounces)

1 medium apple, peeled, cored and chopped

2 tablespoons butter, cut into several pieces

1 tablespoon lemon juice

½ cup sugar

1 sheet frozen puff pastry (half of 17.3-ounce package), thawed according to package directions

A little all-purpose flour for rolling out dough

1 egg, beaten with a fork

2 teaspoons coarse sugar such as turbinado, optional

In heavy-bottomed non-aluminum saucepan, combine blueberries, apple, butter and lemon juice. Heat over medium heat until fruits start to produce juices. Stir in sugar and cook, stirring frequently, until sugar dissolves and mixture is bubbling, about 3 minutes. Adjust heat so mixture is gently boiling and cook, stirring occasionally, until mixture is thick and no longer runny, about 15 minutes. Remove from heat and set aside until no longer hot, then refrigerate for at least an hour, or until cold (filling can be prepared a day in advance; transfer mixture to a bowl, then cover tightly and refrigerate until needed).

When you're ready to bake, heat oven to 400°F. Line a rimmed baking sheet with kitchen parchment. On lightly floured worksurface, roll puff pastry to a 12x12-inch rectangle; cut in half to make two 6x12-inch rectangles. Place 1 rectangle on prepared baking sheet; set aside. Sprinkle top of remaining rectangle with a little flour, then fold in half the long way (3x12 inches). Cut a slit about 1½ inches long in the middle of the sheet, cutting from the folded edge towards the outer edge. Cut 2 more slits on each side of the center slit (for a total of 5 slits), spacing the slits about 1¾ inches from the center slit and from each other; see diagram below.

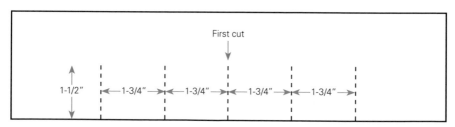

First cut

1-1/2"　　1-3/4"　1-3/4"　1-3/4"　1-3/4"

Spoon cold blueberry mixture onto pastry that is on the baking sheet, leaving a 1-inch border. Brush border lightly with beaten egg. Place second pastry on top, aligning the uncut edge with one of the long edges of the bottom pastry. Unfold the pastry, aligning the edges; the slits should open slightly, revealing the filling. Press all edges together very well with a fork. Brush entire top of pastry with beaten egg, then sprinkle with the coarse sugar. Bake until golden brown, 25 to 30 minutes. Cool on baking sheet until lukewarm before using two large spatulas to transfer pastry to serving plate. Cut along the slits to serve.

 Plan your schedule so you can prepare the filling at least an hour before you plan to bake the tart; it needs to be cold when the tart is assembled. Apples help thicken the blueberry filling.

Blueberry Filling
About ½ cup; easily increased

½ teaspoon water

½ teaspoon cornstarch

6 ounces fresh or previously frozen blueberries (about 1⅓ cups)

1 heaping tablespoon grated apple

1 tablespoon sugar

In small bowl, blend together water and cornstarch; set aside. In small, heavy-bottomed saucepan, combine blueberries, apple and sugar. Crush fruit gently with a potato masher to start juices flowing. Heat to boiling over medium-high heat, then cook, stirring frequently and mashing once more, until mixture is no longer runny; this will take 8 to 10 minutes. Add cornstarch mixture, stirring constantly; cook for about 1 minute longer, or until thick. Cool before using.

Use this to prepare Easy Bear Claws (pg. 20), Fruit-Striped Cookie Fingers (pg. 119), or Fruit-Filled Muffins (pg. 146). Refrigerate extra filling, and use to top oatmeal or toast.

Wild Blueberry Pancakes

9 pancakes

When wild blueberries are on the breakfast menu, it's worth taking the few extra minutes to whip up a homemade batter.

1 cup whole milk

1½ teaspoons freshly squeezed lemon juice

1 cup plus 2 tablespoons all-purpose flour

1 tablespoon powdered sugar

1¼ teaspoons baking powder

¼ teaspoon salt

2 tablespoons unsalted butter, melted and cooled slightly

1 egg

Nonstick cooking spray (or vegetable oil)

⅔ cup fresh blueberries (about 3 ounces)

Butter and syrup for serving

In 2-cup measure, stir together milk and lemon juice; set aside while you prepare the other ingredients. Begin heating a griddle over medium heat.

Place a wire-mesh strainer over a mixing bowl. Add flour, powdered sugar, baking powder and salt to strainer; shake to sift into bowl. Add butter and egg to milk; beat with a fork until well-blended. Pour all at once into flour mixture; stir with the fork until batter is just combined. Don't over-mix; there should be a number of small lumps in the batter.

Spray hot griddle with nonstick spray (or brush with vegetable oil). Pour batter in ¼-cup batches onto griddle. Immediately scatter about 1 tablespoon of blueberries over each pancake. Cook until bottom is nicely browned and spotted, and top side has numerous small bubbles beginning to appear. Flip carefully and cook second side until spotted with brown. Transfer to a warm serving plate; cover loosely and keep warm while you cook remaining pancakes. Serve hot, with butter and syrup.

Variation: To use frozen berries, substitute ⅔ cup frozen blueberries for the fresh berries. While berries are still frozen, place them into a wire-mesh strainer and rinse them briefly under cool water, then spread out in a single layer on a paper towel to dry while you prepare the batter.

 Adding the berries to the pancake once it's on the griddle prevents soggy purple pancakes. This technique also works beautifully with wild strawberries.

Blueberry Spirals with Cardamom

8 rolls

Cardamom adds an unusual touch to these rolls. Plan on eating these with a knife and fork, to get every bit of the delicious berry filling.

1 loaf (1 pound) frozen bread dough, thawed according to package directions

All-purpose flour for rolling out dough

2 tablespoons butter, softened

1 cup fresh blueberries (about 4½ ounces)

½ cup chopped pecans

3 tablespoons sugar

½ teaspoon ground cardamom

¼ teaspoon cinnamon

Spray an 8x12-inch baking dish with nonstick spray; set aside. Roll bread dough on lightly floured worksurface to a rectangle about 8 inches by 12 inches. Spread butter evenly over bread. Sprinkle blueberries and pecans over bread, keeping an inch away from the long edges. In a small bowl, stir together the sugar, cardamom and cinnamon; sprinkle evenly over bread. Starting with a long edge, roll up bread, jelly-roll fashion; as you roll, tuck the blueberries in if they pop out. Press the dough together at the long edge once the dough is rolled. Cut into 8 even slices. Place in prepared baking dish with a cut side up; there will be a fair amount of space between the rolls. If some of the berries or nuts fall out, tuck them into the spirals. Cover with plastic wrap and let rise at room temperature for about an hour.

Near the end of the rising time, heat oven to 350°F. Uncover rolls; bake until cooked through, 35 to 40 minutes; cover dish with foil during the last 10 minutes of baking if rolls are browning too quickly. Remove from oven, and remove foil if used. Let rolls cool for about 5 minutes, then cover with foil, bringing it down the sides of the dish. Place a baking sheet over the dish, and (using potholders) quickly but carefully flip everything over together. Remove the baking dish. Let cool at least 15 minutes before eating; best served warm and fresh.

This recipe was developed for use with wild blueberries, which are much smaller than domestic blueberries. If domestic blueberries are substituted, the rolls have big gaps because the berries are too large!

Gravel Pie with Dried Blueberries   1 pie (6 to 8 servings)

Here's an adaptation of an old Pennsylvania Dutch specialty, originally prepared with raisins. It's unique, very sweet—and really good.

1 cup (packed) golden brown sugar

½ cup hot water

3 eggs

4½ ounces sugar cookies or vanilla wafers

⅔ cup all-purpose flour

½ teaspoon cinnamon

¼ teaspoon nutmeg

⅛ teaspoon ground ginger

½ cup (1 stick) cold butter, cut into pieces

½ cup dried blueberries

**1 pre-baked pie crust, lightly golden
    (see "Blind Baking Pie Crusts", pg. 67)**

Add 2 inches of water to the bottom of a double boiler and heat over medium heat until simmering. In mixing bowl, combine sugar, water and eggs; beat well with whisk. Transfer to top half of double boiler and place over simmering water in bottom half of double boiler. Cook, stirring almost constantly, until thick, 10 to 15 minutes; the mixture should look like thick gravy. Remove top half of double boiler and place on a heat-proof surface; set aside until cool. Near the end of cooling, heat oven to 325°F.

Meanwhile, chop cookies in food processor (or place in a plastic bag and bash them with a rolling pin) until medium-coarse. Measure crumbs; there should be about 1¼ cups. (If you have more than 1¼ cups, reserve additional crumbs for garnishing pudding or other desserts.) In medium bowl, stir together flour, cinnamon, nutmeg and ginger. Add butter; blend together with your fingertips until mixture is crumbly but still coarse.

Sprinkle blueberries in bottom of pie crust. Pour egg mixture evenly into pie on top of blueberries. Sprinkle half of the flour mixture over egg mixture; top with half of the cookie crumbs. Repeat layers. Bake until golden brown and set, 28 to 33 minutes.

No Double Boiler?

If a recipe calls for use of a double boiler, but you don't have one, you can use a large stainless-steel bowl and a saucepan. Heat a few inches of water in the saucepan until simmering. Put the mixture to be cooked in the stainless-steel bowl, then set it on top of the saucepan and proceed as directed.

Old-Fashioned Blueberry Dumplings

4 servings

Many recipes for blueberry dumplings involve a dumpling mixture that is cooked in hot blueberry sauce. This one puts the berries inside, where they fill the dumplings with flavor. These make a wonderful, filling breakfast.

- **1½ cups all-purpose flour, plus additional for rolling out dough**
- **½ cup sugar**
- **1 teaspoon baking powder**
- **½ teaspoon salt**
- **⅜ cup whole or 2% milk**
- **4 tablespoons (half of a stick) unsalted butter, melted and cooled slightly**
- **1 egg**
- **1 cup fresh blueberries (about 4½ ounces)**
- **For serving: milk, butter, and cinnamon-sugar (½ cup sugar mixed with ½ teaspoon cinnamon)**

Start heating a large pot of water to boiling over high heat. Place wire-mesh strainer over mixing bowl. Add 1½ cups flour, the sugar, baking powder and salt; shake to sift into bowl. In measuring cup, combine milk, butter and egg; beat with a fork. Add to flour mixture and stir with wooden spoon until well-mixed.

Transfer dough to lightly floured worksurface and knead a few times. Roll out about ¼ inch thick. Cut into 2-inch squares. Divide blueberries among the squares. Make the dumplings one at a time: Fold corners together over the berries. Work the dough in your hand, squeezing slightly, until you hear or feel the berries popping slightly and the ball of dough is well-sealed. Repeat with remaining dough and berries.

Drop dumplings, a few at a time, into boiling water. Cook, stirring gently if they stick to the bottom of the pot, until dumplings float; cook for about 3 minutes longer after they float. Use slotted spoon to transfer to a bowl; cover and keep warm while you prepare remaining dumplings. Serve warm dumplings in a bowl, with butter, milk and cinnamon-sugar to top.

Cookies with Dried Fruit, Nuts and White Chocolate Chips

About 30 cookies

A nice combination of fruit, nuts and white chocolate.

½ cup (1 stick) unsalted butter, softened

⅓ cup (packed) brown sugar

⅓ cup white sugar

1 egg

1 teaspoon vanilla extract

1 cup plus 2 tablespoons all-purpose flour

½ teaspoon baking soda

½ teaspoon salt

⅔ cup dried blueberries, dried serviceberries, or other dried berries

½ cup white chocolate chips

½ cup chopped pecans

Heat oven to 350°F. Line 2 baking sheets with kitchen parchment, or spray with nonstick spray. Combine butter, brown sugar and white sugar in mixing bowl; beat with electric mixer until light. Add egg and vanilla; beat well. Place wire-mesh strainer over bowl. Add flour, baking soda and salt; shake strainer to sift mixture into bowl. Stir with wooden spoon until well mixed. Add dried blueberries, chocolate chips and pecans; mix well (mixture will be stiff). Roll into walnut-sized balls, placing 1½ inches apart on prepared baking sheets. Bake for 7 minutes, then rotate pans (see "Rotating Cookies while Baking," pg. 9). Continue baking until golden brown, 9 to 12 minutes longer; centers will still be soft. Cool on baking sheets for 2 minutes, then transfer to wire rack to cool.

Variation: Substitute "berries" made with autumn olive or other fruit purée (pg. 8) for the dried blueberries. Before sifting the flour into the butter mixture, transfer a tablespoon of the flour to a medium bowl. Add the "berries" and stir to coat with flour. Proceed as directed, adding the floured "berries" with the white chocolate chips and nuts.

 Egg Talk

Recipes in this book simply call for "eggs" without distinguishing between sizes. For best results, use large eggs, rather than medium or small eggs. If you are watching cholesterol, you may substitute ¼ cup liquid egg substitute for each egg in a recipe; it works great in place of whole eggs in all dishes except custards.

Blueberry-Maple Breakfast Casserole 6 to 8 servings

A little preparation the night before lets you put a wonderful, warm breakfast together with ease. The maple syrup is a perfect complement to the blueberries.

1 loaf (1 pound) French bread, cut into ½-inch cubes

8 ounces cream cheese, cut into ½-inch cubes (reduced-fat works fine)

1 to 1½ cups fresh or previously frozen blueberries (4½ to 7 ounces)

8 eggs

2½ cups whole milk

½ cup real maple syrup

½ teaspoon salt

Spray 9x13-inch baking dish with nonstick spray. Distribute half of the bread cubes in the dish. Top with cream cheese cubes and blueberries, distributing evenly; top with remaining bread cubes. In large mixing bowl, beat together eggs, milk, syrup and salt until smooth. Pour evenly over bread. Cover and refrigerate overnight.

The next morning, heat oven to 350°F. Uncover dish; bake until top is golden brown and center is set, 35 to 45 minutes. Let stand 10 minutes before serving.

Other recipes in this book featuring blueberries, bilberries and huckleberries:
Colorful Fruit Salad, pg. 30
Overnight Multi-Grain Cereal with Fruit and Nuts, pg. 59
Serviceberry or Blueberry Freezer Jam, pg. 134
Fruits of the Forest Pie, pg. 156
Dehydrating Wild Berries and Fruits, pgs. 168–169
As a substitute in Refrigerator Cookies with Dried Berries, pg. 9
As a substitute in Blackberry-Apple Crisp, pg. 15
As a substitute in Individual Currant Cheesecakes, pg. 57
As a substitute in Serviceberry Pudding Cake, pg. 138
As a variation in Thimbleberry Smoothie, pg. 152

Quick ideas for using blueberries, bilberries and huckleberries:
Use fresh, wild blueberries, huckleberries or bilberries in any
recipe you have that calls for fresh blueberries.

BUNCHBERRIES *(Cornus canadensis)*

The bright red fruits of this plant are a charming sight in the forest, but they don't do much to get the forager excited. Although edible, the fruits are basically tasteless. One advantage this diminutive fruit does offer is that it is high in pectin. When making jam with fruits such as blueberries that lack natural pectin, bunchberries can be added to help thicken the jam naturally. They can also be used in cooked cereals, muffins and quick breads, to add bulk and thickening—if not much taste.

Bunchberries make an acceptable trail nibble—more for the sake of novelty than anything else—and are also good to know about as a survival food.

Colorful Fruit Salad

4 servings

Here, bunchberries add color and texture to a fruit salad that is brimming with flavor from the other fruits. Use wild or domestic blueberries and raspberries, depending on what you have on hand.

1 cup blueberries

1 cup raspberries

1 cup cut-up pineapple (canned or fresh)

1 cup seedless red or green grapes, halved

⅓ cup bunchberries

1 kiwi fruit, peeled and cut up

1 orange, peeled, seeded and cut up

2 teaspoons sugar

Combine all ingredients in a large mixing bowl. Stir gently. Let stand at room temperature for at least 15 minutes, and as long as 1 hour, before serving.

PIN CHERRY, BLACK CHERRY, CHOKECHERRY and SAND CHERRY
(Prunus pensylvanica, P. serotina, P. virginiana and P. pumila)

Wild cherries are tart but delicious; quality varies from tree to tree, but juice from all of them makes an exceptional, sparkling jelly. Pin cherry jelly is often regarded as one of the finest of the wild jellies; be sure to give it a try. The flesh of pin cherries, chokecherries and black cherries is thin in proportion to the pits; sand cherries are meatier, and can be pitted with a regular cherry pitter to make pie or other baked goods.

Don't crush the pits of any of these fruits during cooking or straining. Cherry pits contain small amounts of a cyanide-forming compound that can cause illness if eaten in large quantities.

Black cherries are the most difficult to harvest, because the fruit is out of reach in the tall trees; sand cherries are the easiest, as they are a low shrub that bears heavily. Pin cherry trees bear a lot of fruit, but it's tough to beat the birds to them; however, the fruit hangs low and a good deal can be gathered from the ground—if you're there at the right time. Chokecherries are easy to pick because the plants are lower-growing and produce plentiful fruit; also, the fruit grows in long clusters so it's easy to pull off a big handful rather than picking one fruit at a time. Note that two varieties of chokecherry grow in our area: the common chokecherry (*P. virginiana*) which is dark red when ripe, and the black chokecherry (*P. virginiana* v. *melanocarpa*), which is black when ripe. Both can be used interchangeably in recipes.

Juice and purée prepared from all four species of cherries listed here are interchangeable, so all recipes in this section simply call for wild cherry juice, rather than listing all four species in each recipe. The only recipe that is not interchangeable is Sand Cherry Pie (pg. 35), which really does need to be made with sand cherries—unless you have the patience to remove the pits from a gallon of, say, chokecherries.

To prepare purée or juice, measure the fruit and place in a non-aluminum pot. For purée, add 1 cup water per quart of fruit; for juice, add 2 cups water per quart of fruit. Heat to boiling, then reduce the heat; cover and simmer for about 30 minutes, gently crushing the fruit with a potato masher near the end of cooking. **For purée,** process the cooked fruit through a cone-shaped colander, then discard the pits. **For juice,** transfer the mixture to a strainer lined with doubled, dampened cheesecloth and let it drip for 30 minutes; if you're making jelly, don't squeeze the fruit or the jelly will be cloudy. After the clear liquid has dripped away, set it aside and squeeze the fruit into a different container; you can use this slightly cloudy juice as a beverage or for cooking. Processed this way, a quart of fruit will yield about 1 cup of purée (slightly more for sand cherries), or about 1½ cups juice.

Wild Cherry Zabaglione

This light, fluffy dessert is an adaptation of zabaglione (zah-bye-LYOH-neh), a classic Italian dessert which is typically made with Marsala or other sweet wine. Serve it with shortbread cookies, or topped with fresh fruit such as raspberries.

1 cup whipping cream

2 tablespoons plus ⅓ cup sugar, divided

½ teaspoon vanilla extract

5 egg yolks

⅓ cup wild cherry juice

In large mixing bowl, combine cream, 2 tablespoons sugar and the vanilla. Beat with electric mixer until stiff. Refrigerate until needed.

Add 2 inches of water to the bottom of a double boiler that has a large top half;* heat over medium heat until simmering. In top half of double boiler, combine egg yolks and remaining ⅓ cup sugar. Beat with electric hand mixer until fluffy and light-colored. Add cherry juice; beat with mixer until well combined. Place top half of double boiler over the bottom half so the egg mixture in the top half will be heated by the simmering water in the bottom half. Cook, beating constantly with electric mixer, until mixture is thick and holds soft peaks, 8 to 10 minutes. Remove top half of double boiler and place on a heat-proof surface; continue beating for 3 or 4 minutes. Let stand until completely cool, about 10 minutes. Add to mixing bowl with whipped cream, gently folding together with rubber spatula. Refrigerate for 30 minutes, or as long as 2 hours. Serve in parfait glasses.

*If you don't have a double boiler, or the top half on yours is small, see "No Double Boiler?" on pg. 26.

If you have leftovers, transfer them to a freezer-safe container and freeze for at least 8 hours; the frozen zabaglione becomes an airy, delicious ice cream.

Cherry Wigglers

32 or 64 candies, depending on shape

These gelatin squares are firm enough to be carried in a lunchbox for several hours without melting in all but the hottest weather.

1¾ cups wild cherry juice, divided

2 envelopes unflavored gelatin

½ cup sugar

Spray an 8-inch-square baking dish with nonstick spray; set aside. Place ½ cup of the cherry juice in a small bowl; sprinkle gelatin on top and set aside. In non-aluminum saucepan, combine remaining 1¼ cups cherry juice and the sugar. Heat to boiling over medium-high heat and cook, stirring constantly, until mixture boils and sugar dissolves, about 3 minutes. Scrape gelatin mixture into saucepan; stir until the gelatin dissolves. Remove from heat and cool for about 5 minutes, then pour into prepared dish. Let cool at room temperature for about 15 minutes, then cover with plastic wrap, pressing the wrap against the surface of the mixture. Refrigerate until firm, about 3 hours. Cut into long, skinny fingers or 1-inch squares, as you prefer; store in the refrigerator in a tightly sealed plastic container with plastic wrap between the layers.

Wild Cherry Jelly

4 half-pints

2½ cups wild cherry juice

2 tablespoons lemon juice

Two-thirds of a 1.75-ounce box powdered pectin

½ teaspoon butter, optional (helps reduce foaming)

2¾ cups sugar

Prepare and process as directed in Jelly Instructions (using pectin), pg. 164.

Homemade Cherry Cordial

The black cherry is sometimes called rum or whisky cherry because it was often used in the past to make a flavored liqueur. Here's a version of that for you to try.

2 cups whole wild cherries

1½ cups vodka

1½ cups brandy

2 strips orange zest, each about ½ inch wide and 1 inch long (colored rind only, with none of the white pith)

4 whole cloves

⅓ cup sugar

⅓ cup water

½ teaspoon glycerin (from the drugstore)

Sterilize a 1-quart canning jar, lid and band as directed on pg. 171. In large bowl, gently crush cherries with a potato masher; pick out and discard pits, squeezing over the bowl to extract any flesh or juice. Transfer cherries and juice to sterilized jar. Add vodka, brandy, orange zest and cloves. Seal jar with sterilized lid and shake well. Set in a cool, dark spot for 4 weeks, shaking occasionally.

At the end of 4 weeks, strain mixture through cheesecloth-lined strainer into a clean bowl; press on the cherries to extract the liquid. Discard the solids. Line a funnel with a paper coffee filter. Strain liquid into a clean, sterilized 1-quart canning jar; set aside.

In small saucepan, combine sugar and water. Heat over medium-low heat, stirring frequently, until sugar dissolves and liquid is clear. Remove from heat; set aside until completely cool. Strain syrup through a clean coffee filter into the jar with the cordial. Add glycerin; seal jar and shake to blend. Let stand, tightly sealed, for 2 or 3 days before serving; store in a cool, dark place for up to 3 months.

Zesting Citrus Fruits

The "zest" is the colored part of the rind only, with none of the bitter white pith. Always wash the fruit well before zesting.

__To make zest strips,__ use a very sharp knife to cut off the colored part of the rind, being careful to avoid getting any of the white pith.

__To make grated zest,__ the best tool is a microplane grater; this rasp-like tool looks like it belongs in a woodworker's shop, but it really is superior for grating zest. Hold the grater over a small bowl with the teeth facing up, and draw the fruit over the teeth. When you start to see the lighter part of the rind, rotate the fruit and grate in a fresh spot. If you don't have a microplane grater, use the fine holes on a box grater, or a porcelain ginger grater.

Wild Cherry-Lemonade Sparkler

1 quart; easily increased

This tangy, refreshing beverage goes down well when the mercury heads skyward.

1½ cups wild cherry juice

¾ cup freshly squeezed lemon juice

½ cup sugar, or to taste

1 can (12 ounces) lime-flavored carbonated water

In serving pitcher, combine cherry juice, lemon juice and sugar; stir to dissolve sugar. Add carbonated water; pour over ice in tall glasses. Note: If you don't want to serve all of the sparkler at once, mix the cherry juice, lemon juice and sugar first, then add to sparkling water as each drink is served.

Sand Cherry Pie

1 pie (6 to 8 servings)

2½ cups pitted sand cherries, plus juice that collects during pitting

⅓ cup white sugar

⅓ cup (packed) dark brown sugar

3 tablespoons minute tapioca

⅛ teaspoon almond extract, optional

Ready-to-use pastry for single-crust pie

1½ tablespoons butter, cut into small pieces

Heat oven to 425°F. In mixing bowl, combine cherries, juices from pitting, white and brown sugars, tapioca and almond extract. Stir well; let stand for 15 minutes. Meanwhile, line pie plate with pastry and flute edges decoratively; set aside until needed.

When cherries have rested for 15 minutes, scrape into prepared pie plate. Dot with butter. Place on baking sheet (to catch drips) and bake for 10 minutes; reduce heat to 350°F and bake until filling thickens and bubbles and crust is golden brown, about 30 minutes longer. Serve warm or at room temperature.

 Pit the cherries over a mixing bowl to collect all the precious juice.

Cherry Barbecue Sauce

About 1 cup

This works well with just about any grilled meat, but is particularly good on game such as duck and goose.

1¼ pounds whole wild cherries, stems removed

⅓ cup orange juice

¼ cup chopped shallot

1 tablespoon minced fresh gingerroot

½ teaspoon ground cumin

½ teaspoon freshly ground black pepper

1 small hot red pepper, stem and seeds removed

2 tablespoons tomato paste

2 tablespoons white wine vinegar

¾ teaspoon salt

In heavy-bottomed non-aluminum saucepan, combine cherries, orange juice, shallot, gingerroot, cumin, black pepper and hot pepper. Heat to boiling over medium heat, then cook, stirring occasionally, until most of the liquid has cooked away, about 20 minutes. Remove from heat and cool slightly, then process through food mill. Transfer purée to smaller heavy-bottomed non-aluminum saucepan; add tomato paste, vinegar and salt. Simmer over medium-low heat for 20 minutes, stirring occasionally; if sauce is thinner than you like, increase heat slightly and cook until reduced as much as you like.

If a recipe calls for a small quantity of tomato paste, you can freeze the rest of the can in small portions for future use. Drop the extra paste, in 1-tablespoon mounds, onto a piece of waxed paper set on top of a plate. Freeze until solid, then roll up the waxed paper with the tomato mounds, and store in a freezer container. Next time you need a tablespoon of tomato paste, simply unroll the waxed paper and peel off a tablespoon; it will thaw quickly, and be ready to use in a jiffy.

Easy Cherry Applesauce

This fast and easy applesauce is cooked in the microwave. Cherry purée provides a lovely color, and a delightfully tangy flavor.

3 cups sliced apples (peeled, cored and sliced before measuring)

½ cup sugar, or as needed

⅔ cup wild cherry purée

½ teaspoon cinnamon

¼ teaspoon nutmeg

A good pinch of ground cardamom

Combine all ingredients in microwave-safe mixing bowl. Cover with waxed paper. Microwave on high/100% power for 10 minutes or until apples are soft, stirring once halfway through. Cool apple mixture slightly, then mash to desired consistency with potato masher. Taste, and add additional sugar if necessary (stir the sugar into the warm sauce, and heat briefly in the microwave to incorporate the sugar). Serve warm or chilled.

Use Fireside, McIntosh, Granny Smith or other cooking apples; if you have a windfall of large crabapples, you can use them, but it's a lot of work to peel and core 3 cups of crabapples!

Other recipes in this book featuring wild cherries:
Six Recipes Using Wild Fruit Juice or Syrup, pgs. 158–162
Wild Berry or Fruit Syrup, pg. 163
As a substitute in Pumpkin Tart with Currant Glaze, pg. 60
As a variation in Fruit Terrine with Elderberry Gel, pg. 64
As a variation in Elderberry Meringue Pie, pg. 66
As a substitute in Spicy Plum Chutney, pg. 141

CHOKEBERRIES or ARONIA *(Aronia melanocarpa)*

Most wild-foods books sold in the United States don't even mention chokeberries. They're much more common in central and eastern Europe, where they typically go by the more flattering name aronia. The juice is used as a beverage, and the fruits are combined with apples to make wine.

Unlike chokecherries and many other fall fruits, chokeberries contain no inedible stone or large, annoying seeds. They grow in abundance on the shrubs, so it's easy to gather a good quantity. Chokeberries have a sweet flavor, but the flesh has an acrid quality that will leave your mouth feeling dry, similar to the effect of eating an underripe apple or a raw cranberry. The juice makes an excellent jelly or syrup, with no acrid feeling at all.

Aronia juice is considered a health food, because the fruits are rich in anthocyanins, a phytonutrient that may lower blood pressure and protect against circulatory problems caused by diabetes.

To prepare purée or juice, measure the chokeberries. Chop coarsely in a food processor (the fruit will stain any white parts of the processor, by the way), and place in a non-aluminum pot. For purée, add 1 cup water per quart of fruit (measured before chopping); for juice, add 2½ cups water per quart of fruit. Heat to boiling, then reduce the heat; cover and simmer for about 20 minutes. **For purée,** process the cooked fruit in the food processor again, until it is the desired texture. **For juice,** transfer the mixture to a strainer lined with doubled, dampened cheesecloth. Rinse the cooking pot with 1 cup of water, and pour that into the strainer with the other fruit. Let it drip for 30 minutes, then gently squeeze the cheesecloth bundle to extract more juice (your hands will turn purple, and remain that way for a day or two). Processed this way, a quart of chokeberries will yield about 2 cups of very dark pulp, or about 3 cups of rich, purplish-black juice; if your yield of juice is less, add water to make up the difference. Chokeberries may be frozen by following the instructions for blueberries on pg. 18.

Aronia Jelly

4 half-pints

2⅓ cups chokeberry juice

2 tablespoons lemon juice

Two-thirds of a 1.75-ounce box powdered pectin

½ teaspoon butter, optional (helps reduce foaming)

2½ cups sugar

Prepare and process as directed in Jelly Instructions (using pectin), pg. 164.

Chokeberry-Cornmeal Cake

The topping on this rustic cake is similar to that on caramel rolls—except it's dark purple! This cake is best on the day it's made; the caramelized topping gets soft overnight.

Topping:

3 tablespoons butter

¾ cup (packed) brown sugar

1¼ cups fresh or previously frozen chokeberries (about 6¼ ounces)

½ cup (1 stick) butter, softened

¾ cup white sugar

2 eggs

⅓ cup sour cream

1 teaspoon vanilla extract

1 cup all-purpose flour

½ cup cornmeal

1½ teaspoons baking powder

¼ teaspoon salt

Cut a square of kitchen parchment to fit the bottom of an 8-inch-square baking dish. Spray dish with nonstick spray; place parchment in bottom, smoothing in place. Set aside. Make the topping: In small saucepan, melt butter over medium heat. Add brown sugar and cook, stirring constantly, until smooth. Add chokeberries; increase heat to medium-high and cook, stirring occasionally, until mixture comes to a boil. Cook, stirring frequently, for about 3 minutes. Remove from heat and set aside until cool. Heat oven to 350°F.

In large mixing bowl, beat butter with electric mixer until smooth and light. Add white sugar; beat until fluffy. Add eggs one at a time, beating after each addition. Add sour cream and vanilla; beat well. Place wire-mesh strainer over the mixing bowl. Add flour, cornmeal, baking powder and salt; shake to sift into bowl. Fold in with rubber spatula until just moistened. Pour cooled berry mixture into prepared pan. Spoon batter evenly into baking dish over berry mixture, spreading gently; it will not be flat but that's okay. Bake until top is light brown and springs back when touched lightly, 40 to 50 minutes. Transfer pan to wire rack and let cool for 10 minutes, then run a table knife around the edges to loosen. Place a flat platter (or small sheet pan) on top of the pan and carefully invert the two together; remove baking dish. Remove parchment. Let cool for at least 30 minutes before serving; serve warm or at room temperature.

Pear and Chokeberry Mincemeat

Use this filling to make a delicious mincemeat pie; warm the filling up and serve over ice cream or pound cake; or use in any recipe calling for mincemeat.

2 pounds ripe but firm Anjou, Bartlett or other pears (about 4 Anjou)

⅔ cup fresh or previously frozen chokeberries (about 4 ounces)

2 tablespoons freshly squeezed lemon juice

⅔ cup sugar

¾ cup water, divided

2 teaspoons corn syrup

½ cup golden raisins

¼ cup dried cranberries

½ teaspoon cinnamon

½ teaspoon allspice

¼ teaspoon nutmeg

¼ teaspoon salt

¾ cup chopped pecans, butternuts or hickory nuts (medium-fine)

2 tablespoons rum or brandy, or ½ teaspoon rum extract

2 tablespoons unsalted butter

Peel, quarter and core pears and place in food processor workbowl, cutting each piece into thirds as you add to the workbowl. Add chokeberries and lemon juice, and chop until pears are coarse, with pieces no larger than ½ inch (or, chop fruits by hand, sprinkling afterwards with lemon juice). Set aside.

In heavy-bottomed non-aluminum 4-quart saucepan, stir sugar, ¼ cup water and the corn syrup together. Cook over medium heat, stirring constantly with a wooden spoon, until sugar dissolves and mixture comes to a boil. Continue to cook, stirring occasionally, until mixture turns golden, about 7 minutes; watch carefully, as the syrup colors quite rapidly when it is ready and it's easy to over-brown the syrup. Remove pan from heat and carefully add the remaining ½ cup water, avoiding the steam that will come up from the hot syrup. The syrup will harden when the water is added. Return the pan to medium heat and cook, stirring constantly, until the hardened syrup dissolves. Add pear mixture, raisins, cranberries, cinnamon, allspice, nutmeg and salt. Adjust heat so mixture boils gently. Cook, stirring frequently, until thickened, 45 to 50 minutes.

Add nuts, rum and butter. Cook, stirring frequently, for about 5 minutes. If canning, process immediately as described below; otherwise, cool completely before storing in refrigerator or freezing.

To can Pear and Chokeberry Mincemeat: Follow canning instructions on pg. 171. Pack hot mincemeat into hot pint jars. Process in boiling-water bath for 20 minutes.

 The mincemeat will keep for a week in the refrigerator, and the flavor actually improves after a day or two.

Pear and Chokeberry Mincemeat Pie 1 pie (6 to 8 servings)

For a holiday treat, serve this pie warm with a scoop of vanilla ice cream, or a big dollop of lightly sweetened whipped cream.

Ready-to-use pastry for double-crust pie

3½ to 4 cups Pear and Chokeberry Mincemeat

1½ teaspoons unsalted butter, cut into small pieces

1 egg yolk, beaten with 1 tablespoon cold water

Fit one of the pastries into an ungreased pie plate. Trim edges, leaving ¾ inch overhang. Cover and chill pie crust and remaining pastry dough for 30 minutes.

When pastry has chilled, heat oven to 425°F. Spoon mincemeat into prepared crust; the crust should be comfortably full but not over the edge. Dot top with butter. Moisten edges of pastry in pie plate, then top with second pastry, or make a lattice top as described on pg. 69. Seal, trim and flute edges. Brush top crust with egg wash; if you've used a plain top crust rather than a lattice, cut inch-long slits in the crust in 6 to 8 places for ventilation. Place pie on baking sheet (to catch drips) and bake in center of oven until crust is golden and filling bubbles through vents or lattices, about 25 minutes. Cool to warm room temperature before serving; best served on the day it is made.

Other recipes in this book featuring chokeberries:
Six Recipes Using Wild Fruit Juice or Syrup, pgs. 158–162
Wild Berry or Fruit Syrup, pg. 163

Quick ideas for using chokeberries:
If you're a winemaker, experiment with a chokeberry-apple wine; it's often sold in Europe and is reportedly delicious.
Chokeberry juice can be used in any recipe calling for chokecherry, wild cherry or elderberry juice.

CRABAPPLES *(Malus* spp.)

Numerous varieties of crabapple grow in our region; although size, shape and color vary dramatically, all are edible. Larger fruits, ¾ inch across or more, work best for making purée, or for cutting up to use in recipes; tiny crabapples have a lot of seeds in comparison to the amount of flesh, and it's next to impossible to remove the seeds without destroying the fruit. However, tiny crabapples can be used to make juice; the high proportion of skin makes the juice a particularly deep pink color. Large crabapples can be used to make juice also, but since they are more versatile, you may wish to save them for recipes that call for cut-up fruit.

Crabapples are found just about everywhere, from urban parks and forests, to abandoned fields, to woodlots and shelterbelts. They're easy to identify, and all are edible.

Crabapples, especially those that are slightly underripe, are rich in natural pectin; the juice can be used to make jelly without the commercial pectin needed for most jellies. Even though the juice may look a bit cloudy, the jelly will be clear as long as you don't squeeze the fruit during juicing.

To prepare crabapple juice, cut crabapples in half, removing stems and blossom ends; if fruit has soft spots or bugs, cut away and discard the affected portions. Place in non-aluminum pot; add water to cover crabapples completely. Heat to boiling over high heat. Reduce heat so mixture is simmering, then cover and simmer without stirring until crabapples are very soft, 20 to 25 minutes. Transfer the mixture to a strainer lined with doubled, dampened cheesecloth and let it drip for 30 minutes; if you're making jelly, don't squeeze the fruit or the jelly will be cloudy. After the liquid has dripped away, set it aside and squeeze the fruit into a different container; you can use this cloudy juice as a beverage or for cooking. Yield varies quite a bit, because crabapples vary so much in size; in general, you'll get 2 cups of juice per pound of crabapples.

If you have a fruit press, you can use it to make fresh apple cider from crabapples. You may want to mix in some regular cider apples with the crabapples, to balance the flavor. Home-pressed cider is a delicious beverage on its own, and can also be fermented to make an outstanding wine or hard apple cider. For more information on making wine or hard cider, consult a book on home winemaking such as *First Steps in Winemaking* by C.J.J. Berry or *The American Cider Book* by Vrest Orton.

Crabapple Jelly (no added pectin)

About 3 half-pints per 2 pounds of fruit

Crabapple jelly has a lovely pink color, and a pleasant flavor.

Crabapple juice

1 teaspoon lemon juice for each cup of crabapple juice

⅔ cup sugar for each cup of crabapple juice

Because this recipe does not use commercial pectin, it's more flexible; you can make as little as 2 pints, or as much as 5 pints, depending on how many crabapples you've got. When preparing the juice, use a mix of ripe and slightly underripe fruit for the best flavor and texture. Please read "Jelly Instructions for Fruits with Natural Pectin" on pg. 166 to learn about testing for doneness.

Measure the juice; for each 2 cups of juice, prepare 3 half-pint canning jars, bands and new lids as directed on pg. 171. Place measured juice and lemon juice in a non-aluminum pot that holds at least four times the amount of juice you're using. For each cup of juice, measure ⅔ cup of sugar; set it aside. Heat juice to boiling over medium-high heat. Add sugar and cook, stirring constantly, until sugar dissolves. Increase heat to high and cook, skimming off any foam and stirring frequently, until jelly passes one or more of the doneness tests on pg. 166; this typically takes 10 to 15 minutes.

Once the jelly is done, skim any foam off the surface and pour it, while still hot, into the prepared canning jars; seal with prepared lids and bands. Process in a water-bath canner (pg. 171) for 10 minutes, or store in the refrigerator.

Variation: Add a handful of fresh mint leaves to the crabapples when preparing the juice, for a delightful Crabapple-Mint Jelly.

Make some extra jelly when crabapples are in season, to use as holiday gifts. Cut a square of colorful fabric, large enough to cover the top of the canning jar; wrap it over the lid and tie in place with some pretty ribbon.

Crabapplejack

Traditional applejack is a brandy that has been distilled from apple juice. Here's an easy way to make apple-flavored brandy.

2 cups small crabapples

1 fifth brandy

½ cup sugar, or to taste

You'll need a glass jar that holds at least 40 ounces, with a mouth wide enough to insert the crabapples; juice is often sold in these types of bottles. Wash it very well, then fill it with boiling water and let stand for at least 5 minutes.

Wash crabapples very well; remove stems and blossom ends. Drain water from bottle; add crabapples and brandy. Cap bottle, and place in a cupboard or other dark location that is room temperature or slightly cooler. Let steep for 8 to 10 weeks, gently shaking the bottle once or twice a week.

After the 8- to 10-week period, strain out and discard crabapples. Filter the brandy through a funnel lined with a paper coffee filter into a clean bottle; add sugar. Return the bottle to the cupboard, and let mellow for a few weeks before serving.

Crabapples that are too small to use for baking work well here; the high ratio of skin gives the Crabapplejack a lovely, reddish-gold color.

Crabapple Filling

Cinnamon and brown sugar give a wonderful flavor to this easy filling.

1 cup cored, chopped crabapples (see note below for preparation tips)

1½ tablespoons lemon juice

1½ tablespoons (packed) brown sugar

⅛ teaspoon cinnamon

In small, heavy-bottomed non-aluminum saucepan, combine crabapples and lemon juice. Cover and cook over medium heat, stirring frequently, until crabapples are tender, about 5 minutes. Stir in brown sugar and cinnamon; cook for about a minute longer to dissolve sugar. Cool before using.

Use this to prepare Easy Bear Claws (pg. 20), Fruit-Striped Cookie Fingers (pg. 119), or Fruit-Filled Muffins (pg. 146). Refrigerate extra filling, and use to top oatmeal or toast.

 To prepare the crabapples, cut each crab into quarters. Cut out the core, also removing the stems and blossom remnants; chop cleaned quarters by hand or in a mini food processor.

Crabapple-Ginger-Cardamom Jam

5 half-pints

Sparkling, bright red and tangy, this jam is a favorite of all who try it.

2 pounds crabapples

1 piece peeled fresh gingerroot, about 1" x 3" or slightly larger

3 ⅓ cups sugar

2 cups water

2 tablespoons freshly squeezed lemon juice

¾ teaspoon cardamom seeds (from about 15 cardamom pods)

Prepare 5 half-pint canning jars, bands and lids as directed on pg. 171. Cut crabapples into quarters; remove and discard cores. If crabapples are ½ inch in diameter or smaller, no further preparation is necessary; if crabapples are larger, cut each quarter in half from top to bottom so you have narrower wedges. Place crabapple wedges in heavy-bottomed non-aluminum pan. Grate gingerroot and add to pan along with remaining ingredients.

Heat to boiling over medium-high heat, stirring frequently. Reduce heat so mixture is bubbling at a moderate pace and cook, stirring frequently, until thickened, 45 minutes to 1 hour; a small scoop of jam should jell as described in Green Gooseberry Jam on pg. 70. Ladle into prepared jars, leaving ½ inch headspace. Seal with prepared lids and bands. Process in boiling-water bath for 10 minutes.

Other recipes in this book featuring crabapples:
>Highbush-Apple Leather, pg. 94
>Six Recipes Using Wild Fruit Juice or Syrup, pgs. 158–162
>Wild Berry or Fruit Syrup, pg. 163
>Dehydrating Wild Berries and Fruits, pgs. 168–169
>As a substitute in Autumn Olive "Berries" for Baking, pg. 8
>As a substitute in Easy Cherry Applesauce, pg. 37
>As a substitute in Hawthorn and Sausage Brunch Casserole, pg. 87
>As a substitute in Rose Hip-Apple Jelly, pg. 128

Quick ideas for using crabapples:
>Crabapple juice mixes well with other wild fruit juices for making jelly.

CRANBERRY *(Vaccinium macrocarpon and others)*

Three varieties of wild cranberry are found in our region; other than size differences, they are quite similar to each other and to commercially grown cranberries. Like the commercial variety, wild cranberries can be eaten raw, but they are quite tart. They are more commonly cooked, or ground and enhanced with orange juice and sugar to make a relish.

To prepare cranberry juice, measure the fruit. Chop coarsely in a food processor, and place in a non-aluminum pot. Add 2½ cups water per quart of fruit. Heat to boiling, then reduce the heat; cover and simmer for about 10 minutes. Transfer the mixture to a strainer lined with doubled,

Wild cranberries can be used exactly as you would use purchased cranberries, although fruits of the wild species are typically a bit smaller.

dampened cheesecloth and let it drip for 30 minutes; if you're making jelly, don't squeeze the fruit or the jelly will be cloudy. After the clear liquid has dripped away, set it aside and squeeze the fruit into a different container; you can use this slightly cloudy juice as a beverage or for cooking. Processed this way, a quart of fruit will yield about 3 cups of bright red juice.

Cranberries freeze well; simply spread them out on a baking sheet and freeze overnight, then pack into freezer-weight plastic bags or other containers. They can be dehydrated and eaten out of hand as a snack; home-dehydrated fruits can also be used in recipes calling for craisins.

Turkey Breast with Cranberry Pan Sauce   4 servings

Here's a nice way to fix turkey breast, complete with the traditional cranberry accent; it would even work for an intimate Thanksgiving dinner.

1 to 1¼ pounds sliced, uncooked turkey breast (½-inch-thick slices)

⅓ cup all-purpose flour

1 teaspoon paprika

½ teaspoon salt

¼ teaspoon pepper

1 tablespoon butter

1 tablespoon olive oil

¼ cup finely minced red onion

2 cloves garlic, finely chopped

½ teaspoon crumbled dried rosemary

½ cup Port or other rich, sweet red wine

2 tablespoons balsamic vinegar

1¼ cups chicken broth

⅔ to ¾ cup fresh or previously frozen cranberries

1 tablespoon cornstarch

1 tablespoon cold water

Pat turkey slices dry with paper towels. In food-storage bag, combine flour, paprika, salt and pepper; shake to mix. Add turkey slices; shake to coat. Transfer turkey slices to plate, shaking off excess flour. In large skillet, melt butter in oil over medium heat. Add turkey breast slices in a single layer. Cook until lightly browned on both sides and no longer pink inside, about 4 minutes per side. Transfer to clean plate; cover and set aside.

Add onion, garlic and rosemary to same skillet (if it seems to be too dry, add a little more olive oil). Sauté over medium heat for about a minute. Add port and vinegar; increase heat to high. Heat to boiling and cook for about 2 minutes, stirring frequently. Add broth and cranberries; return to boiling. Reduce heat to a gentle boil and cook for about 5 minutes, stirring frequently. Blend together cornstarch and water in a small bowl. Add about half of the cornstarch mixture to the sauce. Increase heat slightly and cook, stirring constantly, until sauce thickens and bubbles; if necessary, add additional cornstarch mixture. When sauce is thickened, reduce heat to medium. Return turkey slices and any accumulated juices to skillet. Cook until heated through, 2 to 3 minutes.

Wild Rice with Cranberries and Nuts

This is a wonderful side dish to serve with any type of roast; it also goes well with pork chops or venison steaks.

1 tablespoon butter or oil

Half of an onion, diced

½ cup chopped pecans, hazelnuts or walnuts

¾ to 1 cup fresh or previously frozen cranberries

**1½ cups hand-harvested, hand-finished wild rice
(see note below if using commercially grown wild rice)**

1 quart low-sodium chicken broth

In small skillet, melt butter over medium heat, or heat oil until hot but not smoking. Add onion; cook for about 5 minutes, stirring occasionally. Add nuts; cook for 5 minutes longer. Stir in cranberries; remove from heat and set aside

Rinse wild rice very well to remove any dust or foreign matter. In medium saucepan, combine rice and chicken broth. Heat to boiling over medium-high heat, then reduce heat and boil gently until rice is just starting to get tender, about 10 minutes. Add onion-cranberry mixture. Continue cooking until rice is tender and grains have plumped a bit, generally 5 to 10 minutes longer; if rice becomes too dry, stir in a little hot water as needed. When rice is done, cover and remove from heat; let stand for about 5 minutes, then fluff and serve.

Note: If you're using paddy-grown, commercial wild rice, you may need to cook it as long as 45 minutes before it becomes tender; add additional water if needed for the longer cooking.

Wild-grown, hand-harvested and hand-finished genuine wild rice is very different from commercially bred, paddy-grown "wild" rice. It's nuttier, with a more complex flavor, and it cooks more quickly. Commercial "wild" rice is darker and harder; it takes much longer to cook, and has a flavor that seems muddy by comparison. If you're using hand-finished wild rice in a recipe that was written for the commercial variety, start checking for doneness after 15 minutes; because it doesn't need to cook as long, it usually needs less water, too. (On the other hand, if you're using commercial rice in a recipe that was developed for truly wild rice, plan on cooking it as long as an hour, adding additional water as necessary.) A good source for hand-harvested, hand-finished wild rice is the White Earth Land Recovery Project at nativeharvest.com.

Cranberry Jelly (for spreading)

5 half-pints

This sparkling-clear, bright red jelly is great on toast.

3 cups cranberry juice

2 tablespoons lemon juice

Half of a 1.75-ounce box powdered pectin

½ teaspoon butter, optional (helps reduce foaming)

3½ cups sugar

Prepare and process as directed in Jelly Instructions (using pectin), pg. 164.

Cranberry Jelly (for slicing)

2 pints

This is a more solid jelly that is meant to be turned out of the jar, then sliced. Serve it with poultry, pork or venison.

2½ cups cranberry juice

2 tablespoons lemon juice

3-ounce pouch liquid pectin

½ teaspoon butter, optional (helps reduce foaming)

3 cups sugar

Prepare and process as directed in Jelly Instructions (using pectin), pg. 164.

When ready to serve, place the jar in a pot of very hot water (enough to come up to the level of jelly in the jar); let stand for about 5 minutes. Slide the jelly out onto a plate; if it resists, run a table knife around the edges. Cut into ¼-inch-thick slices.

 Use wide-mouth pint canning jars, with sides that slope outward from the base. The jelly should slide out easily.

Cranberry Bread

3 mini-loaves, or 1 standard-sized loaf

Small loaves of this moist, tangy bread make much-appreciated holiday gifts.

2 navel oranges, well washed

1 cup plus 3 tablespoons sugar, divided

1¼ cups fresh cranberries

¾ cup walnut pieces

½ cup (1 stick) unsalted butter, softened

1 egg

1½ teaspoons baking powder

½ teaspoon baking soda

½ teaspoon salt

2 cups all-purpose flour

Heat oven to 350°F. Spray 3 mini-loaf pans, or 1 standard-sized loaf pan, with nonstick spray; dust with a little flour and set aside. From one of the oranges, cut 2 strips of zest (colored rind only, with none of the white pith), about ½ inch wide and 2 inches long. Add zest to food processor along with the 3 tablespoons sugar. Process until very fine. Add cranberries; pulse on-and-off until chopped to medium texture. Transfer to a small bowl. Add nuts to food processor (no need to clean the processor first); pulse a few times until chopped, then add them to the bowl with the cranberries and set aside.

In mixing bowl, combine butter and remaining 1 cup sugar. Beat with an electric mixer until light and fluffy, about 2 minutes. Add egg; beat until light. Add baking powder, baking soda and salt; beat well. Squeeze the oranges, then measure ¾ cup juice; reserve remaining juice for other uses. Add the measured juice and the cranberry mixture to the butter mixture; stir with wooden spoon to combine. Add flour; stir until just moistened (do not over-mix or the bread will be tough). Divide batter evenly between prepared loaf pans. Bake until loaf is springy and brown, and a toothpick inserted in the center comes out clean; mini-loaf pans take about 50 minutes, while a standard loaf pan takes about an hour. You may leave the bread in the pans if you've got decorative foil pans and plan to give them away; otherwise, cool for 10 minutes, then turn out to complete cooling.

Fresh Cranberry Relish

About 1½ cups

This uncooked relish has a wonderful sweet and tangy taste. Serve it in a glass bowl to show off the lovely color.

1 navel orange, well washed

1 cup sugar

1 cup fresh cranberries

1 Granny Smith or other tart apple

From half of the orange, use a sharp paring knife to remove the zest (colored rind only, with none of the white pith), cutting it in strips. Add to food processor, along with sugar. Process until zest is finely chopped. Peel orange, and divide into halves; wrap and refrigerate one half for other uses. Divide remaining orange half into sections and remove any seeds. Add orange sections and cranberries to food processor. Peel and core the apple, then cut into 1-inch chunks. Add to food processor. Pulse on-and-off in very short bursts, scraping down the sides of the workbowl, until mixture is chopped to a medium consistency; don't over-process. Transfer to a glass or ceramic bowl; let stand at room temperature for an hour to allow sugar to dissolve and flavors to blend.

Variation: Add ¼ cup pecan halves to the fruit before processing.

My mother-in-law tells of making fresh cranberry relish when she was growing up on a farm in western Minnesota. They used a hand-cranked meat grinder to chop the fruit. If you have a meat grinder, give it a try with this recipe (use the medium plate); the texture is very nice.

Other recipes in this book featuring cranberries:
Pear and Chokeberry Mincemeat, pg. 40
Overnight Multi-Grain Cereal with Fruit and Nuts, pg. 59
Spicy Gooseberry-Apple Crisp, pg. 74
Oatmeal Muffins with Russian Olive, pg. 132
Six Recipes Using Wild Fruit Juice or Syrup, pgs. 158–162
Wild Berry or Fruit Syrup, pg. 163
Dehydrating Wild Berries and Fruits, pgs. 168–169

Quick ideas for using cranberries:
Use in any recipe that calls for commercial cranberries.
Sweeten the juice to taste, and serve as a breakfast drink or an appetizer; it's also good when blended with apple or other juice.

CREEPING OREGON GRAPE *(Mahonia repens)*

Fruits from the creeping Oregon grape are quite tart, with a slightly bitter overtone; they make a wonderful jelly. They are often pressed with apples and fermented to make a lovely, rose-colored wine (usually called Mahonia wine).

To prepare juice from creeping Oregon grapes, measure the fruit and place in a non-aluminum pot. Add enough water to just cover the fruit. Heat to boiling, then reduce the heat; cover and simmer for about 15 minutes, gently crushing the fruit with a potato masher about midway through the cooking. Transfer the mixture to a strainer lined with doubled, dampened cheese-cloth and let it drip for 30 minutes; if you're making jelly, don't squeeze the fruit or the jelly will be cloudy. After the clear liquid

Some botanists feel that most Mahonia species should be categorized in the barberry family (Berberis) because the plants look very similar and some members of these two groups can hybridize with each other.

has dripped away, set it aside and squeeze the fruit into a different container; you can use this slightly cloudy juice as a beverage or for cooking. Processed this way, a quart of fruit will yield about 2½ cups of lovely, bright purplish juice. Some cooks like to use apple juice, or a mix of apple juice and water, when preparing juice from creeping Oregon grape.

Oregon Grape Jelly
4 half-pints

2½ cups creeping Oregon grape juice

Half of a 1.75-ounce box powdered pectin

½ teaspoon butter, optional (helps reduce foaming)

3½ cups sugar

Prepare and process as directed in Jelly Instructions (using pectin), pg. 164.

Other recipes in this book featuring creeping Oregon grapes:
Six Recipes Using Wild Fruit Juice or Syrup, pgs. 158–162
Wild Berry or Fruit Syrup, pg. 163

CURRANTS *(Ribes* spp.*)*

Several varieties of currant are found in our area; all can be used in the same way, although their taste varies quite a bit. They can be eaten raw, although most are fairly tart. When properly prepared, however, their tartness accents other flavors; they work well in savory dishes as well as sweet. Flavor varies from plant to plant; before harvesting a large quantity, taste them to be sure they will work for your uses. Red currants tend to be sweeter than black ones, but this is not a hard-and-fast rule.

Currants grow in racemes, long clusters containing multiple fruits. Snip off the entire cluster rather than trying to pick the fruits off individually, unless the fruits have ripened unevenly. At home, wash the clusters and pull individual berries off the stemlets. If you're using them whole for baking or other dishes, also remove the dried flower remnant at the bottom; if you're making juice, don't bother with this step. Currants have small seeds that are noticeable but not objectionable; however, some people prefer to cook the fruit and strain it to remove the seeds.

Ripe currants retain their quality even if they are left on the plant for a week or more; I usually find, however, that birds and other critters have beaten me to the berries once they're ripe, so don't wait too long to harvest them.

To prepare currant juice, measure the fruit and place in a non-aluminum pot. Add ½ cup water per quart of fruit. Gently crush the fruit with a potato masher to start the juices flowing. Heat to boiling, then reduce the heat; cover and simmer for about 10 minutes. Transfer the mixture to a strainer lined with doubled, dampened cheesecloth and let it drip for 30 minutes; if you're making jelly, don't squeeze the fruit or the jelly will be cloudy. After the clear liquid has dripped away, set it aside and squeeze the fruit into a different container; you can use this slightly cloudy juice as a beverage or for cooking. Processed this way, a quart of fruit will yield about 2 cups juice.

Currants freeze well. Wash them and remove the blossom remnant, then either spread in a single layer on a baking sheet and freeze overnight, or pack into containers in measured amounts and freeze. If you've frozen them on a baking sheet, pack the frozen berries into containers and store in the freezer; you can measure out what you need and return the rest to the freezer. Currants are also a good choice for drying; note that the fruit sold in the store as "dried currants" is actually a dried grape, so your home-dried currants will be quite different.

Currant-Basil Sauce

About ½ cup sauce, enough for 4 servings

Basil adds a sweet, grassy note to the tangy currants in this savory sauce. Serve it over grilled or poached fish such as salmon or trout; it's also delicious with grilled pork tenderloin or chops.

2 tablespoons finely chopped shallots

1 teaspoon olive oil

¼ cup seasoned rice vinegar

2 tablespoons dry, fruity red wine, such as Tempranillo or Beaujolais

2 tablespoons finely chopped fresh basil leaves

1 teaspoon sugar

¾ cup fresh red or black currants (about 4 ounces)

1 tablespoon unsalted butter

Salt and pepper

In small skillet, sauté shallots in oil over medium heat for about 3 minutes. Stir in vinegar, wine, basil and sugar. Cook until liquid reduces by half, 3 to 5 minutes. Add currants; cook, stirring occasionally, until the mixture is saucy, about 5 minutes. Remove from heat; add butter and stir until melted. Season to taste with salt and pepper. Spoon warm sauce over prepared fish or pork.

Salted vs. Unsalted Butter

Many recipes in this book call specifically for unsalted butter. I have long believed that some creameries use fresher cream to make unsalted butter than that which is used for salted butter, because fresher cream is less likely to have "off" flavors, which salt helps cover in less-fresh, salted butter. Even if both types of butter are made from the exact same cream, unsalted butter has a fresher, cleaner taste than salted butter.

If a recipe calls for unsalted butter, you may substitute salted butter, but should reduce any added salt a bit to make up for the extra salt in the butter. If a recipe doesn't specifically call for salted or unsalted butter, feel free to use the type you have on hand; if you tend to like saltier food, then salted butter is a good choice, but if you're watching sodium intake, unsalted butter is a better option.

Red Currant and Blue Cheese Butter

About ½ cup, enough for 8 servings

This is outstanding when melted atop a freshly grilled steak; try it with grilled venison for an extra-special treat.

½ cup (1 stick) unsalted butter, softened

¼ cup red currants (about 1¼ ounces)

1 small clove garlic, pressed

4 ounces blue cheese, crumbled

In mixing bowl, combine butter, currants and garlic. Mash with a fork until well-combined. Add blue cheese and mash lightly to combine; some of the blue cheese should retain its texture. Spoon mixture onto a piece of waxed paper, in a line about 8 inches long. Roll up the waxed paper tightly, forming a cylinder; twist the ends closed. Refrigerate for at least 2 hours, or as long as 5 days. To serve, slice off 1-inch-long pieces; place on hot steaks that are fresh from the grill or broiler.

 For longer storage, wrap the butter roll in foil and freeze. It will keep for several months in the freezer; you can slice off what you need from the frozen roll and return it to the freezer.

Currant Jelly

4 half-pints

3 cups currant juice

Half of a 1.75-ounce box powdered pectin

½ teaspoon butter, optional (helps reduce foaming)

3¼ cups sugar

Prepare and process as directed in Jelly Instructions (using pectin), pg. 164.

Individual Currant Cheesecakes 10 mini cheesecakes

Here's a fun recipe for picnics or parties ... individual cheesecakes studded with colorful currants. The graham cracker crust adds nice texture.

1 tablespoon butter

6 squares graham crackers (about 1¾ ounces), finely crushed

1 package (8 ounces) cream cheese, softened

¼ cup sugar

1 egg

1 teaspoon vanilla extract

1 cup fresh red or black currants (about 5½ ounces)

You'll also need: 10 foil baking cups (cupcake liners made of foil)

Heat oven to 350°F. Use foil baking cups to line 10 standard-sized muffin cups. In small microwave-safe bowl, melt butter. Stir in crushed graham crackers. Divide evenly between baking cups (about 1 tablespoon per cup); set aside.

In mixing bowl, combine cream cheese and sugar. Beat with electric mixer until smooth. Add egg and vanilla; beat until well combined. Add currants; stir in gently with a spatula. Divide mixture evenly between prepared baking cups. Bake for about 30 minutes, or until just set and tops are beginning to turn golden brown. Cool to room temperature; refrigerate for at least 4 hours before serving.

Substitutions: Use serviceberries, blueberries or ripe gooseberries in place of the currants, or use a mix of these fruits. Frozen berries may also be used; defrost before using.

Pears Poached in Spiced Currant Juice   4 servings

Currant juice combines with pears for a delicious dessert. It would also be perfect on a brunch table.

2 firm but ripe Bosc or Anjou pears

1½ cups red currant juice

½ cup ruby Port wine

3 tablespoons honey

1 cinnamon stick

2 whole cloves

A few strips of orange zest (colored rind only, with none of the white pith)

Ice cream or whipped cream for serving

You'll need a heavy-bottomed 2- to 3-quart non-aluminum saucepan to prepare this; before starting, cut a round of kitchen parchment that will fit snugly inside the saucepan. Peel pears, cut in half lengthwise and scoop out the seed core with a melon baller or teaspoon.

In saucepan, combine currant juice, Port, honey, cinnamon stick, cloves and orange zest. Heat to boiling over medium-high heat. Reduce heat so mixture simmers. Add pears; cover with kitchen parchment, pressing it directly onto the pears (this wicks the liquid up over the pears, making the color uniform). Simmer, turning occasionally and replacing the parchment, until pears are just tender, about 25 minutes. Transfer pears to a ceramic or glass mixing bowl.

Increase heat to medium-high and cook until liquid is syrupy; this will take 5 to 15 minutes. Use a wire-mesh strainer to strain reduced liquid over pears, discarding spices; set pears aside until completely cool, about 45 minutes. (The pears can be poached a day in advance; cover and refrigerate, but bring them to room temperature before serving.) Serve pears cut-side down, with syrup poured around; top each pear with a small scoop of ice cream or some whipped cream.

Aluminum and Non-Aluminum Cookware
Citrus juices, such as lemon or lime juice, are obviously high in acid, but even wild fruit juices have some acid. Aluminum reacts with acid to create undesirable flavors; the acid also dissolves minute particles of aluminum into the food, which may be a health concern. Many recipes in this book call for the use of non-aluminum cookware. Stainless-steel and Pyrex are good choices; this type of cookware is sometimes called "non-reactive" because it doesn't react with acids.

Overnight Multi-Grain Cereal with Fruit and Nuts
Bulk recipe

This is a wonderful mix to keep on hand. With just a few minutes' prep in the evening, you'll have hearty, cooked breakfast cereal in the morning … and no sticky pan to clean up!

¾ cup dried currants, cranberries or blueberries

⅔ cup chopped pecans

½ cup steel-cut (coarse) oatmeal

⅜ cup buckwheat groats

⅜ cup bulgur

¼ cup pepitas (toasted green pumpkin seeds)

¼ cup pearled barley

¼ cup soft wheat berries

2 tablespoons amaranth

Combine all ingredients in a large bowl; mix well with your hands. Store in a tightly sealed canister.

To prepare: The night before, measure ⅓ cup of the mixture per serving. For each serving, place ⅞ cup water and a pinch of salt in a saucepan or pot. Heat water to boiling. Add the measured mix; stir well. Return to boiling, then cover tightly and remove from the heat. Let stand at room temperature overnight. The next morning, the grains and fruit will be tender; heat on the stovetop or in the microwave, and serve with milk, syrup, butter, sugar or whatever you like. If you cook extra, you can keep it in the refrigerator for several days, heating a portion whenever you like.

The mix above is just a suggestion; feel free to alter the ingredients to suit your taste. Look for the grains and other specialty items at a health-food store, or in the bulk bins at co-ops and stores that specialize in natural or organic foods. Other options to consider: millet, spelt, farro, Kamut®, oat groats, flax seed, wheat germ, and any other dried fruit you like.

Pumpkin Tart with Currant Glaze

1 pie (6 to 8 servings)

Currant juice is particularly good with pumpkin pie; the tartness cuts through the richness of the pie filling very well, and the color is lovely.

1 can (15 ounces) pumpkin

8 ounces cream cheese, softened

2 eggs

¾ cup sugar

1 teaspoon rum extract or vanilla extract, optional

1 teaspoon cinnamon

½ teaspoon ground ginger

¼ teaspoon allspice

1 pre-baked pie crust, lightly golden (see "Blind Baking Pie Crusts," pg. 67)

3 cups currant juice

2 tablespoons cornstarch mixed with 2 tablespoons cold water

Heat oven to 350°F. Combine pumpkin and cream cheese in large mixing bowl. Beat with electric mixer until smooth. Add eggs, sugar, extract, cinnamon, ginger and allspice; beat until smooth. Scrape into pre-baked crust, smoothing top. Bake until set, 45 to 60 minutes. Remove from oven and set aside until cool.

While tart is cooling, prepare glaze. Boil currant juice until reduced to 2 cups (see "Reducing Liquid on pg. 121). Stir in cornstarch mixture. Cook, stirring constantly, until thickened and bubbly. Remove from heat; set aside to cool slightly. Pour cooled mixture over tart, spreading and smoothing with back of spoon. Serve at room temperature; refrigerate leftovers.

Substitutions: Use elderberry or wild cherry juice in place of the currant juice; darker juices like these look best with the pie.

Currant Cordial

Offer this delightful cordial to guests as a special after-dinner drink. It's also wonderfully warming to sip while sitting around the fireplace on a cold winter's night.

3 cups currant juice

½ cup sugar

1 cup brandy

2 whole cardamom pods

2 strips orange zest (colored rind only, with none of the white pith), each about ½ inch wide and 2 inches long

You'll need a glass bottle that holds at least 40 ounces to hold the cordial; juice is often sold in these types of bottles. Wash it very well, then fill it with boiling water and let stand for at least 5 minutes.

In non-aluminum saucepan, combine currant juice and sugar; heat to boiling over medium-high heat and cook, stirring constantly, until sugar dissolves. Remove from heat and set aside until cool. Drain water from the prepared glass bottle, then use a funnel to pour the juice into it. Add remaining ingredients. Seal tightly and place in a dark, cool cupboard to mellow for a few weeks before drinking.

A cordial is similar to a liqueur, but with a lower alcohol content. If you make this cordial with red currant juice, it's a lovely garnet color; if you use black currant juice, it looks like blackberry brandy.

Other recipes in this book featuring currants:
Six Recipes Using Wild Fruit Juice or Syrup, pgs. 158–162
Wild Berry or Fruit Syrup, pg. 163
Dehydrating Wild Berries and Fruits, pgs. 168–169

Quick ideas for using currants:
If the currants are sweet, serve them raw in a bowl topped with thick cream and lots of sugar.
Add dried currants to hot cereal when cooking. Delicious.

ELDERBERRIES, COMMON *(Sambucus canadensis)*

Elderberries have a somewhat musty flavor when sampled raw, but cooking improves the taste, especially when lemon juice is added. Don't taste more than one or two raw, though; many people get an upset stomach from raw elderberries. The seeds also cause digestive problems for some people; if you make an elderberry pie with whole berries, try just a small portion until you are sure you won't have a problem with the seeds.

Pick elderberries by snipping the entire fruit cluster off; place them in a bucket until you have as many as you need. The small stemlets that remain attached to the berries taste bad and can also cause digestive problems. The berries should be pulled off the stemlets soon after picking, because once the stemlets start to wilt, they are more difficult to remove. I rinse the clusters as soon as I get home, then just pull the berries off with my fingertips (which are soon stained purple). Some foragers prefer to place the clusters on a rimmed baking sheet that is propped up on one end, then use a fork to rake the berries off the clusters.

Flowers of the common elderberry can be steeped to make a tea, which is often recommended to relieve headaches. The flower cluster can also be battered and fried to make interesting fritters.

To prepare elderberry juice, measure the stemmed fruit and place in a non-aluminum pot. Add 1 cup water per quart of stemmed fruit. Heat to boiling, then reduce the heat; cover and simmer for about 5 minutes. Crush gently with a potato masher, then simmer for about 5 minutes longer. Transfer the mixture to a strainer lined with doubled, dampened cheesecloth and let it drip for 30 minutes; squeeze once or twice to extract more juice (elderberry juice is so dark that you won't have to worry about the jelly being cloudy if you squeeze the fruit). Processed this way, a quart of fruit will yield about 2 cups juice.

Whole elderberries freeze very well; place measured amounts of stemmed berries in freezer-weight plastic bags or plastic containers, label with the amount, and freeze. Elderberries are also easy to dry, and can sometimes be found in this form at winemaking supply stores. In addition to being used in winemaking, dried elderberries are used in baked goods, although if you want to try this, keep in mind that the seeds will still be in the dried fruit. To reconstitute dried elderberries, simply cover them generously with warm water and let stand until plumped up. A few reconstituted elderberries added to a batch of muffins, or to an apple pie, will make a delicious and different dessert. The soaking liquid can be added to other fruit juice for an interesting beverage.

Elderberry Jelly

4 half-pints

2½ cups elderberry juice

3 tablespoons lemon juice

Two-thirds of a 1.75-ounce box powdered pectin

½ teaspoon butter, optional (helps reduce foaming)

2¾ cups sugar

Prepare and process as directed in Jelly Instructions (using pectin), pg. 164.

Elderberry-Sumac Jelly

4 half-pints

Elderberry jelly is delicious on its own, but sumac juice raises it to another level. This is one of the finest wild jellies you can make. The idea for this delightful combination comes from the late Euell Gibbons, in his book Stalking the Wild Asparagus.

3 cups stemless fresh elderberries, or 1 cup dried

2½ cups strained sumac juice (pg. 148)

Two-thirds of a 1.75-ounce box powdered pectin

½ teaspoon butter, optional (helps reduce foaming)

2¾ cups sugar

In non-aluminum saucepan, combine elderberries and sumac juice. Heat to a gentle boil. If using fresh elderberries, cook for 5 minutes, then crush gently with potato masher and cook for 5 minutes longer. If using dried elderberries, cook for 10 minutes, then remove from heat and let stand for 20 minutes.

Transfer the mixture to a strainer lined with doubled, dampened cheesecloth and let it drip for 30 minutes; squeeze once or twice to extract more juice. Measure the juice; add water if necessary to bring it up to 2½ cups. Prepare and process as directed in Jelly Instructions (using pectin), pg. 164.

Fruit Terrine with Elderberry Gel

6 to 8 servings

This combines elderberry juice with fresh, purchased fruits for a truly lovely dessert—a clear gel glistening with fruits.

2 tablespoons cold water

2 tablespoons plain gelatin

1 cup elderberry juice

1 cup apple juice

½ cup sugar

1 cup cut-up peaches (fresh or previously frozen), cut into ½-inch pieces before measuring

1 cup fresh raspberries (wild or domestic)

1 cup whole, seedless green grapes (smaller grapes work best here)

A small amount of whipped cream for garnish, optional

Place cold water in a small bowl; sprinkle gelatin over the top. Let stand until gelatin softens, about 5 minutes. While gelatin is softening, in medium saucepan, combine elderberry juice, apple juice and sugar. Cook over medium heat, stirring constantly, until sugar dissolves, about 5 minutes. Remove from heat. Scrape softened gelatin into fruit juices; stir until gelatin is dissolved, 2 to 3 minutes. Cool to lukewarm.

While juice mixture is cooling, arrange peaches, raspberries and grapes in standard-sized glass loaf pan. Pour lukewarm fruit juice mixture over fruits; if any fruit is floating, press it down into the juice. Cover pan with plastic wrap and refrigerate until set, at least 3 hours; terrine can be prepared up to a day in advance.

To serve, run about 2 inches of hot water into the sink, then hold the pan in the sink so the water is level with the top of the gel; let stand in the hot water for about 15 seconds to loosen. (If it isn't loose along the sides, run a table knife between the gel and the pan.) Place a serving plate on top of the loaf pan and invert the two together, holding the plate and pan together tightly. Shake the pan slightly if necessary to release the terrine. Use a very sharp knife to slice crosswise into 6 to 8 pieces; top each serving with a small dollop of whipped cream, if you like.

Variation: Substitute juice from wild cherries or chokecherries for the elderberry juice. Increase sugar to ⅔ cup.

Elderberry Liqueur

About 1 quart

This lovely purple liqueur can be served straight in a cordial glass, or on the rocks.

2 cups stemmed fresh elderberries

2 cups water

¾ cup sugar

2 cups vodka

¼ cup freshly squeezed lemon juice

1 teaspoon anise seeds

You'll need a glass bottle that holds at least 40 ounces to hold the liqueur during its steeping period; juice is often sold in these types of bottles. Wash it very well, then fill it with boiling water and let stand for at least 5 minutes.

In blender or food processor, chop elderberries coarsely. In non-aluminum saucepan, combine water and sugar. Heat to boiling over medium-high heat, stirring constantly until sugar dissolves and mixture is clear. Add chopped elderberries; reduce heat to low and cook for 5 minutes, stirring occasionally. Remove from heat and set aside until cool. Drain water from glass bottle, then use a funnel to pour mixture into it. Add vodka, lemon juice and anise seeds. Seal tightly and place in a dark, cool cupboard for 2 to 3 weeks, shaking the bottle every day or two.

After steeping for 2 or 3 weeks, strain the mixture into another clean bottle through a strainer lined with a double layer of cheesecloth; discard mixture in cheesecloth. Refrigerate strained liquid for 8 hours or longer, to allow any sediment to settle. Pour clear liquid into a clean 1-quart bottle through a funnel lined with a paper coffee filter. For best quality, store in refrigerator.

 To make an elderberry martini, combine 2 parts elderberry liqueur with 1 part gin in an ice-filled cocktail shaker; shake and strain into a chilled martini glass. Garnish with a curl of lemon zest.

Elderberry Meringue Pie

This pie looks so pretty, with the dark purple filling and fluffy meringue. It also looks like you spent all day slaving over it, but really, it's quite easy to make.

1 cup plus 1 tablespoon sugar

5 tablespoons cornstarch

⅛ teaspoon salt

1 cup elderberry juice

½ cup water

4 egg yolks

2 tablespoons butter

½ cup freshly squeezed lemon juice

**1 pre-baked pie crust, lightly golden
(see "Blind Baking Pie Crusts," pg. 67)**

<u>Meringue:</u>

4 egg whites*

½ teaspoon vanilla extract

¼ teaspoon cream of tartar

½ cup sugar

Heat oven to 350°F. In medium non-aluminum saucepan, stir sugar, cornstarch and salt together. Whisking constantly, stir in elderberry juice and water. Cook over medium-high heat, whisking constantly, until mixture boils; reduce heat to low and cook, whisking constantly, about 3 minutes longer. Remove from heat.

In small bowl, beat egg yolks lightly with a fork. Add ½ cup of the warm elderberry mixture to the egg yolks; beat with fork until smooth. Whisk egg yolk mixture into elderberry mixture. Return to medium-high heat and cook, whisking constantly, until thick, 3 to 4 minutes. Remove from heat. Add butter; whisk until dissolved. Add lemon juice; whisk until well blended. Scrape mixture into pre-baked pie crust; set aside while you prepare the meringue.

Prepare the meringue: In very clean mixing bowl, combine egg whites, vanilla and cream of tartar. Beat with electric mixer until soft peaks form. Gradually add sugar, beating continuously; continue beating until mixture is glossy and stiff peaks form. Spoon mixture over filling in crust, spreading all the way to the edges of the filling to seal to the crust;

use a spoon to pull some of the meringue up into peaks. Bake for 12 to 15 minutes, or until golden brown. Cool before serving.

*Use egg whites from pasteurized eggs if concerned about salmonella. You may also be able to purchase cartons of pasteurized egg whites, sold specifically for use in recipes such as meringue, at larger supermarkets.

Variation: Substitute juice from wild cherries or chokecherries for the elderberry juice; increase sugar to 1¼ cups. Or, substitute highbush cranberry juice for the elderberry juice; increase sugar to 1⅔ cups.

Blind Baking Pie Crusts

Sometimes, a recipe calls for a pre-baked pie crust. Here's how to make one. Place the rolled-out pastry dough into a pie plate; flute the edges decoratively. Place a large piece of foil inside, pressing it into the corners. Fill the foil with uncooked dry beans; if you do a lot of baking, you can also buy aluminum pie weights for this purpose at specialty cookware stores. Bake at 375°F for 10 minutes. Remove from oven. Carefully lift the foil by the corners, folding it in to contain the beans; place it in a mixing bowl and set it aside. Return the pie crust to the oven. For recipes that will get additional baking, bake until firm and very lightly golden, about 10 minutes; for recipes that will get little or no additional baking, bake until golden brown, about 15 minutes. Let crust cool before filling, or as directed in recipe.

The beans can no longer be used for bean recipes, but they can be saved for use when blind baking pies in the future; simply cool them completely, then transfer to a heavyweight plastic bag and store in the cupboard until you need them.

Other recipes in this book featuring elderberries:

Wild Berry Vinegar, pg. 13
Six Recipes Using Wild Fruit Juice or Syrup, pgs. 158–162
Wild Berry or Fruit Syrup, pg. 163
Dehydrating Wild Berries and Fruits, pgs. 168–169
As a substitute in Pumpkin Tart with Currant Glaze, pg. 60

Quick ideas for using elderberries:

Elderberry wine is often considered to be one of the best of the wild fruit wines, but it requires a lot of berries—and the stemlets need to be removed before you start. If you want to try making it, check out *Progressive Winemaking* by Peter Duncan and Bryan Acron.

Use the whole berries to make a pie, following any recipe you've got for blueberry pie; reconstituted dried berries are particularly good for pie. As noted on page 62, eat only a very small portion of this pie until you know you're not going to have a reaction to the seeds.

GOOSEBERRIES *(Ribes spp.)*

Four types of gooseberries grow in our area: Missouri, prickly, Canadian and smooth. Fruits from these species taste about the same, so they all work for any gooseberry recipe. Gooseberries are unusual because the fruit can be used in its green stage as well as when fully ripe. They have a tart, refreshing flavor, somewhat reminiscent of rhubarb; ripe gooseberries are sweeter than green ones. Green gooseberries are rich in pectin, so they can be used to make jam without adding commercial pectin; they also make a good pie filling, because the pectin helps thicken the juices naturally.

When picking green gooseberries, choose those that are close to full size, about ⅜ inch across; they will still be firm, but will begin to appear slightly translucent around the edges. Taste one before picking a lot (unless you're picking prickly gooseberries, which are too spiny to taste raw). If the berry is hard and tastes acrid, the gooseberries are underripe; wait a week or so before picking. As summer progresses,

Yes, those fierce-looking prickly gooseberries are edible! The spines are fairly soft, so picking them isn't painful (except for the thorns that grow on the stems). Cooking softens the prickles, making them unnoticeable.

you'll see gooseberries in all stages of ripeness on the plant at the same time, and you'll quickly get a feel for judging the correct stage.

Gooseberries grow abundantly on the plants, and you'll often find plants in small colonies, so it's easy to pick a good quantity. The work starts once you get them home, because you'll need to remove the stems and the "pigtail," a withered brown flower remnant at the base of the berry (if you're juicing the fruit, you don't need to remove the stems or tails). To clean green gooseberries, use a very sharp paring knife to slice off the stem and all parts of the pigtail. A knife works best on green gooseberries, which are firm enough to allow slicing. Once gooseberries ripen, the pressure of the knife and your fingertips tends to mangle the berries; sharp scissors work better (or pinch the stems and tails off with your fingernails).

To make gooseberry juice, place washed gooseberries in a small non-aluminum soup pot (you don't need to remove the stems or tails). Gently crush the fruit with a potato masher to start the flow of juice. Add ½ cup water per quart of gooseberries. Heat to boiling, then reduce the heat; cover and simmer for about 10 minutes. Transfer the mixture to a strainer lined with doubled, dampened cheesecloth and let it drip for 30 minutes; if you're making jelly, don't squeeze the fruit or the jelly will be cloudy. After the clear liquid has dripped away, set it aside and squeeze the fruit into a different container; you can use this slightly cloudy juice as a beverage or for cooking. Processed this way, a quart of gooseberries will yield about 2 cups of juice.

Gooseberries freeze well. Simply wash them and remove the stems and tails, then freeze in heavyweight plastic food-storage bags or tightly lidded plastic containers.

Green Gooseberry Pie

1 pie (6 to 8 servings)

This is an old-time recipe, from back in the days when every farmhouse had a gooseberry pie cooling on the windowsill during "goosie season."

3½ cups green gooseberries (about 1¼ pounds)

1½ cups sugar

2 tablespoons minute tapioca

**½ teaspoon finely grated orange zest
(colored rind only, with none of the white pith)**

¼ teaspoon nutmeg

¼ teaspoon salt

Ready-to-use pastry for double-crust pie

1½ tablespoons unsalted butter, cut into small pieces

1 egg yolk, beaten with 1 tablespoon cold water

Heat oven to 375°F. In mixing bowl, combine gooseberries, sugar, tapioca, orange zest, nutmeg and salt. Stir gently until well-mixed; set aside for 15 minutes. Meanwhile, fit one pastry into ungreased deep-dish pie plate. Scrape gooseberry mixture into pie plate. Dot with cut-up butter. Moisten edges of pastry in pie plate with a little cold water, then top with second pastry (for the most authentic farmhouse look, make a lattice-top pie; see below). Seal, trim and flute edges. Cut 6 to 8 inch-long slits in the crust. Place pie on baking sheet (to catch drips). Brush top with beaten egg. Bake until crust is golden and filling bubbles through slits, 35 to 40 minutes. Transfer to rack to cool; best served warm, the day it is made.

Making a Lattice-Top Pie

When you're making a pie with a top crust, you can use a lattice top in place of the standard, full top crust; the lattice looks very pretty and homestyle. Here's how.

Fit the bottom crust as usual, and add the filling. Cut the second pastry into ½-inch-wide strips. Position a row of strips, running vertically across the top of the pie and separated by ½ inch. Now begin to weave a row of strips horizontally across the top of the pie, lifting the vertical strips over the horizontal strips in an alternating pattern. Trim all strips even with the edge of the overhanging crust, and pinch all edges very well to seal; flute edge decoratively. Brush with egg wash or any other finish as directed in the recipe; the pie is ready to be baked.

Green Gooseberry Jam (no pectin)

1 cup of cleaned gooseberries yields about ¾ cup jam

Green gooseberries contain enough pectin to make jam; once the berries ripen, commercial pectin (which requires precise proportions of fruit, sugar and pectin to work properly) needs to be added to ensure the proper consistency. Since you don't have to mess with pectin in this recipe, it's easy to make a batch of any size.

Measurements are given for 1 cup of cleaned gooseberries, which is the smallest batch you can cook without scorching; adjust proportionally for the amount of gooseberries you've got.

Note: It takes a bit of time to learn how to cook jam without pectin added. It's better to undercook it; you can always cook it a bit more (even after it's cooled) if it's too thin, but if you overcook it, it will be too stiff to use once it's cooled. Follow the instructions below to get the feel for cooking no-pectin jam.

6 ounces fresh or previously frozen green gooseberries (about 1 cup)

3 tablespoons water

6 ounces sugar (1 cup minus 2 tablespoons)

Half a thin pat of butter

Place a small ceramic plate in the freezer; this will be used for testing doneness of the jam. Place gooseberries and water in a heavy-bottomed non-aluminum saucepan. Heat over medium heat until the water starts simmering, then cover and adjust heat so mixture just boils. Cook, covered, for 10 minutes, or until gooseberries are very soft and water has cooked away.

Mash gooseberries with a potato masher, and place the uncovered saucepan over medium heat. Add about a third of the sugar, stirring constantly with a wooden spoon. Cook, stirring constantly, for about a minute to dissolve the sugar. Then add another third of the sugar and cook, stirring constantly, for another minute. Add the remaining sugar and cook for another minute, stirring constantly until all sugar is dissolved.

When all sugar has dissolved, add butter; increase heat to high. When the mixture comes to a full boil, cook for 5 minutes, stirring constantly with a wooden spoon. Remove jam from the heat to prevent overcooking while you test for doneness. Place a spoonful on the cold plate and return to the freezer for a minute; the jam should hold its shape, without weeping around the edges. If the jam is too thin, return to boiling and cook for another minute or so, then re-test; continue as needed until the consistency is correct. Pour into sterilized half-pint canning jars; refrigerate for storage, or process for 10 minutes in a water-bath canner (see pg. 171 for information on sterilizing jars and canning).

Ripe Gooseberry Jelly

4 half-pints

3 cups gooseberry juice (prepared from ripe gooseberries)

One-third of a 1.75-ounce box powdered pectin

½ teaspoon butter, optional (helps reduce foaming)

3¼ cups sugar

Prepare and process as directed in Jelly Instructions (using pectin), pg. 164.

Green Gooseberry Filling

About ½ cup; easily increased

This deliciously tart filling is a nice counterpoint when used in sweet or rich recipes.

6 ounces fresh or previously frozen green gooseberries (about 1 cup)

3 tablespoons sugar, or as needed

2 tablespoons grated apple

1 tablespoon orange juice

Chop gooseberries coarsely by hand or in mini food processor. Combine chopped gooseberries, sugar, apple and orange juice in small, heavy-bottomed saucepan. Heat to boiling over medium-high heat, then cook, stirring frequently, until mixture is no longer runny and looks like chunky applesauce; this will take 9 to 11 minutes. Taste for sweetness, and add a little more sugar if you like. Cool before using.

Use this to prepare Easy Bear Claws (pg. 20), Fruit-Striped Cookie Fingers (pg. 119), or Fruit-Filled Muffins (pg. 146). Refrigerate extra filling, and use to top oatmeal or toast.

Gooseberry Bread with Crumble Topping
8 to 10 servings

Moist with gooseberries, this bread makes a great breakfast or brunch item.

4 tablespoons (half of a stick) unsalted butter, softened

½ cup (packed) brown sugar

1 egg

2 cups all-purpose flour

½ cup white sugar

1½ teaspoons baking powder

½ teaspoon baking soda

½ teaspoon salt

¾ cup fresh orange juice

1⅓ cups fresh ripe gooseberries (about 8 ounces)

¾ cup chopped pecans

Crumble topping:

2 tablespoons white sugar

1 tablespoon all-purpose flour

¼ teaspoon cinnamon

1½ tablespoons cold butter, cut into small pieces

Heat oven to 350°F. Spray a standard-sized loaf pan with nonstick spray; set aside. In mixing bowl, beat butter, brown sugar and egg together with electric mixer until smooth and creamy. Set a wire-mesh strainer over the mixing bowl. Add flour, white sugar, baking powder, baking soda and salt to strainer. Shake to sift into butter mixture. Stir with wooden spoon until dry ingredients are moistened. Add orange juice; stir until just mixed in (batter will be lumpy). Add gooseberries and pecans; stir to mix. Scrape mixture into prepared loaf pan, smoothing top.

Make the crumb topping: In a small bowl, stir together the sugar, flour and cinnamon. Add butter; use a fork or your fingertips to blend the butter into the sugar mixture, working them together until the mixture is the texture of very coarse sand with some pea-sized particles. Use a spoon to sprinkle the crumb topping over the batter. Bake in the center of the oven for 1 hour, or until a toothpick inserted into the center comes out clean. Place pan on wire rack; remove from pan when cool.

Gooseberry Pudding Cake

Sticky and gooey on the bottom, crispy on top … this is delightful for brunch or dessert.

**2½ cups fresh or previously frozen gooseberries
(green or ripe; about 1 pound)**

Batter:

1⅓ cups all-purpose flour

1 cup sugar

1½ teaspoons baking powder

¼ teaspoon salt

½ cup whole or 2% milk

4 tablespoons (half of a stick) butter, melted and cooled slightly

½ teaspoon vanilla extract

1 egg

Topping:

⅔ cup sugar

2 teaspoons cornstarch

¼ teaspoon cinnamon

⅔ cup boiling water

Heat oven to 350°F. Spray 9-inch-square baking dish with nonstick spray. Scatter goose-berries in dish; set aside.

Prepare the batter: Place wire-mesh strainer over mixing bowl. Add flour, sugar, baking powder and salt; shake strainer to sift into bowl. Add milk, butter and vanilla; beat with electric mixer until smooth. Add egg; beat until well mixed, scraping down sides (batter is thick). Spoon batter evenly over gooseberries, then gently spread to the edges of the pan, covering the gooseberries completely.

Prepare the topping: In small bowl, combine sugar, cornstarch and cinnamon; stir until well mixed. Sprinkle evenly over batter. Gently pour boiling water over the batter. Bake until browned and set, 45 to 50 minutes; a toothpick inserted most of the way down should come out clean (don't stick the toothpick all the way down, because the goose-berry layer is gooey). Cool on wire rack for at least 15 minutes before serving; serve warm or at room temperature.

Spicy Gooseberry-Apple Crisp

9 servings

Gingersnaps make a delightfully different topping on this tasty crisp.

Fruit mixture:

2 large Granny Smith or other tart cooking apples (about 1 pound)

2 cups fresh or previously frozen gooseberries
(green or ripe; about 12 ounces)

¾ cup (packed) brown sugar

½ cup dried cranberries (home-dried wild cranberries,
or purchased craisins)

1 tablespoon cornstarch

½ teaspoon cinnamon

¼ teaspoon nutmeg

⅛ teaspoon salt

Topping:

3 ounces gingersnap cookies (about 12 medium cookies)

¼ cup (packed) brown sugar

¼ cup white sugar

¼ cup all-purpose flour

6 tablespoons cold butter, cut into ½-inch pieces

Heat oven to 375°F. Spray 8-inch-square baking dish generously with nonstick spray. Peel and core apples. Cut into ½-inch pieces; add to baking dish. Add remaining fruit mixture ingredients, stirring to mix. Set aside.

In food processor, chop gingersnaps very coarsely. Add remaining ingredients. Pulse on-and-off a few times until mixture is combined but still somewhat coarse in texture. The chunks of butter and gingersnaps should be in chunks a little smaller than a pea. Sprinkle mixture evenly over fruit in baking dish. Bake until the topping is deep golden brown and the fruit is bubbling, 30 to 40 minutes. Cool for at least 45 minutes before serving; best served the day it is made.

Strawberry-Gooseberry Dessert Sauce

Serve this sauce warm or cold. It's good when used to top pound cake, shortcake, ice cream or waffles and can be used in oatmeal for a sweet flavor booster. You may also enjoy it served simply in a dish; try it warm, perhaps with a dollop of whipped cream.

2 cups fresh or previously frozen gooseberries (green or ripe; about 12 ounces)

¾ cup sugar

⅓ cup orange juice or water

1 teaspoon minced fresh gingerroot, optional

A pinch of ground cloves

1 cup sliced strawberries, wild or domestic

1 tablespoon cornstarch, blended with 2 tablespoons water

In saucepan, combine gooseberries, sugar, orange juice, gingerroot and cloves. Heat to boiling; reduce heat and simmer for 10 minutes, stirring occasionally. Add strawberries; cook for about 3 minutes longer. Stir in cornstarch mixture; increase heat to medium-high and cook, stirring constantly, until mixture boils and thickens. Cool slightly before serving or refrigerating.

 This recipe is delicious when prepared with either green or ripe gooseberries. It has a tangier flavor when prepared with green gooseberries.

Other recipes in this book featuring gooseberries:
Six Recipes Using Wild Fruit Juice or Syrup, pgs. 158–162
Wild Berry or Fruit Syrup, pg. 163
Dehydrating Wild Berries and Fruits, pgs. 168–169
As a substitute in Individual Currant Cheesecakes, pg. 57

Quick ideas for using gooseberries:
Substitute gooseberries for cut-up fresh rhubarb in desserts and other recipes.

GRAPES (Riverbank grapes, *Vitis riparia,* and others)

Wild grapes are easy to pick, and grow in good quantities, so it's easy to harvest a gallon in a short time. Use scissors to snip off the entire cluster, dropping it into an ice cream pail or large bag. A 1-gallon ice cream pail holds about 3 pounds of grape clusters. When you're ready to process the grapes, rinse them well. I pick the grapes off the stems before processing them; bugs often lurk in the clusters, and by stemming the grapes, I eliminate these pests. (If you've got a large quantity of grapes to process or are using a press, simply remove the largest stems.)

You can store grapes in the refrigerator up to a week; make sure the grapes at the bottom don't get crushed by the grapes above them, or they will start to rot.

Wild grapes contain tartrate, a substance that causes crystallization in jelly. It burns your skin after prolonged contact, and also burns your mouth if you eat very many raw grapes. Tartrate is removed during juicing.

To prepare juice, place washed grapes in a clean container. Mash with a potato masher, mashing gently to avoid breaking up the bitter seeds. Transfer the mixture to a strainer lined with a triple layer of dampened cheesecloth. Gather the cheesecloth up around the grapes, and squeeze to extract as much juice as possible. Return the fruit-filled cheesecloth to the strainer and open it up; pour about ½ cup water into the fruit pulp, then re-gather the cheesecloth and squeeze again. Return the fruit-filled cheesecloth to the strainer and let it drip for 30 minutes. (Wear clean rubber gloves, or rinse your hands immediately after squeezing the grapes to wash off the tartrate.)

After the crushed grapes have dripped as much as they will, pour the liquid into clean jar; for each quart of stemmed grapes you started with, you'll have about 1½ cups of juice. Refrigerate for 24 hours; a sediment will develop. Carefully pour off the separated liquid into a clean jar; the sediment is fairly solid, but you should pour slowly to avoid stirring it up, and as soon as it nears the stream of liquid you're pouring, stop. Discard the sediment, which contains the tartrate. The amount of sediment varies; it is typically between one-quarter and one-third the total volume of the freshly pressed juice. So each quart of picked grapes yields 1 to 1¼ cups of finished, deep-purple juice.

Grape Jelly (pectin added)   4 half-pints

2½ cups wild grape juice

Half of a 1.75-ounce box powdered pectin

½ teaspoon butter, optional (helps reduce foaming)

3½ cups sugar

Prepare and process as directed in Jelly Instructions (using pectin), pg. 164.

No-Cook Grape Jelly

Although the pectin mixture is cooked, the juice is never heated, resulting in sparkling-clear jelly with a clean, bright flavor. Jelly making doesn't get much easier than this.

1½ cups wild grape juice

2½ cups sugar

**Half of a 1.75-ounce box powdered pectin
(see pg. 164 for information on dividing pectin)**

⅓ cup plus 1 tablespoon water

Sterilize 3 half-pint jars, bands and new lids as directed on pg. 171, or have clean plastic freezer containers ready (see tip on pg. 16). Combine juice and sugar in glass or Pyrex mixing bowl, stirring to dissolve sugar. Let stand for 10 minutes, stirring occasionally.

In small saucepan, combine pectin and water; stir well (mixture may be lumpy). Heat to a full, rolling boil over high heat, stirring constantly. Cook at a rolling boil for 1 minute, stirring constantly. Pour pectin mixture into juice in bowl. Stir constantly with wooden spoon until sugar is completely dissolved and no longer grainy, about 3 minutes; a few grains may remain, but the mixture should no longer look cloudy (or the jelly will be cloudy).

Pour mixture into prepared jars or containers, leaving ½ inch headspace; cover with clean lids. Let stand at room temperature for 24 hours; the jelly should be set. If it is not set, refrigerate for several days until set before using or freezing; grape jelly may take as long as a week to set. The jelly will keep for 3 weeks in the refrigerator, or it may be frozen for up to a year.

Other recipes in this book featuring wild grapes:
> Six Recipes Using Wild Fruit Juice or Syrup, pgs. 158–162
> Wild Berry or Fruit Syrup, pg. 163

Quick ideas for using wild grapes:
> Blend the juice with apple juice, using one part grape juice to two parts apple juice (or to taste). Sweeten as needed; chill before serving.
> Wild grapes make an outstanding wine when combined with chokecherries; see the recipe and complete instructions in my book, *Abundantly Wild: Collecting and Cooking Wild Edibles in the Upper Midwest.*

GROUND CHERRIES (*Physalis virginiana, P. longifolia* and others)

The *Physalis* family is fairly large, and includes not only ground cherries but tomatillos and the ornamental plant commonly called Chinese lantern. All have a ribbed, papery husk enclosing the fruit, which is a pulpy berry with many soft seeds, rather like a small tomato. You probably won't encounter tomatillos or Chinese lanterns in the wild in our area, just one of the numerous varieties of ground cherry.

In our area, ripe ground cherries range from golden yellow, to orange, to purple; it's important to note that ripe ground cherries are never green or black. If you've picked some ground cherries and they are still greenish, let them ripen on the countertop until they soften and are no longer green. If they remain tinged with green, they shouldn't be eaten; unripe ground cherries are somewhat toxic, as are all other parts of the plant including the papery husk. The husk should be very loose around the fruit as well. If you have fruits with husks that cling tightly, discard these without tasting; they probably aren't ground cherries.

Ground cherries were a favorite of early settlers, but today, the fruit is little known except to foragers and a few country folk who still remember them.

To prepare ground cherries, peel away and discard the papery husk. The berries have a sticky, slightly waxy coating that often holds dust, so they should be rinsed after husking; sometimes, they have dark spots of waxy dirt that can be rubbed off while holding the berry under running water. The seeds in ground cherries are soft and unnoticeable, so they don't need to be removed. A quart of husked ground cherries weighs about 1¼ pounds.

Ground cherries are most commonly cooked into jam or preserves, or used in baked goods such as pies. Most ground cherries can be eaten raw or cooked, although some sources state that smooth ground cherry (*P. longifolia*) should be cooked before eating; I can't verify that in any scientific texts, but wanted to pass it along. Ground cherries keep for several weeks in the refrigerator, and can be frozen for longer-term storage; just pack washed berries into plastic bags or containers and freeze with no further preparation. They also dehydrate well (see pgs. 168–169), and make a nice addition to trail mixes when dried. Ground cherries may cause diarrhea if eaten in large quantities, and persons who are allergic to tomatoes should not eat ground cherries.

Ground Cherry Custard Bars

½ cup (1 stick) butter, softened

1 cup all-purpose flour

¼ cup powdered sugar

1 cup husked, ripe ground cherries (about 5 ounces)

Custard:

½ cup sugar

3 tablespoons all-purpose flour

¼ teaspoon salt

½ cup whole milk

2 tablespoons freshly squeezed lemon juice

1 teaspoon vanilla extract

3 egg yolks

Heat oven to 350°F. In a large bowl, beat butter with electric mixer until light. Add flour and powdered sugar; beat at low speed until well combined (mixture will be crumbly). Press mixture firmly into the bottom and ½ inch up the sides of an 8-inch-square baking dish. Bake 15 minutes. While crust is baking, prepare the filling; if the 15 minutes is up before the filling is ready, remove the crust from the oven and set it aside.

To start on the filling: With a very sharp knife, cut the ground cherries into quarters and set aside. Make the custard: Stir sugar, flour and salt together in a heavy-bottomed non-aluminum saucepan. In measuring cup, combine milk, lemon juice, vanilla and egg yolks; stir with a fork to break up and beat in the egg yolks. Slowly add milk mixture to sugar mixture in saucepan, whisking constantly; whisk until smooth. Cook over medium heat, stirring almost constantly, until mixture thickens, about 5 minutes. Remove from heat; stir in ground cherries.

Scrape custard mixture into baked crust, spreading evenly. Return to oven and bake until custard is set, 30 to 35 minutes. Cool completely; cut into 16 squares.

Chicken Salad with Ground Cherries and Almonds

4 servings

A lovely luncheon dish. Serve with warm biscuits and chilled iced tea.

1 pound cooked chicken breast, diced

2 green onions, chopped

½ cup finely diced celery

¼ cup mayonnaise (reduced-fat works fine)

1 tablespoon chopped fresh tarragon

1 cup husked, ripe ground cherries (about 5 ounces)*

¼ cup olive oil

1 tablespoon white wine vinegar

2 teaspoons orange juice

½ teaspoon Dijon mustard

Salt and pepper

4 to 5 cups tender salad greens

½ cup sliced almonds

In mixing bowl, stir together chicken, onions, celery, mayonnaise and tarragon; set aside (or refrigerate, if preparing in advance).

When you're ready to serve, cut ground cherries into halves; set aside. Prepare salad dressing: In a small jar, combine oil, vinegar, orange juice and mustard; cover and shake vigorously. Add salt and pepper to taste. In a large bowl, toss dressing with greens. Divide greens between 4 salad plates. Top each with one-quarter of the chicken salad, mounding attractively. Scatter ground cherries over the salad; top with almonds. Serve immediately.

*Some sources say that smooth ground cherry (*Physalis longifolia*) should not be eaten raw, so it is best to prepare this with a different species.

 You can prepare the chicken salad mixture in advance and keep in the refrigerator until you're ready to serve; dress the greens and assemble the salad right before serving so the greens stay crisp.

Ground Cherry Pie with Cracker Topping
1 pie (6 to 8 servings)

Here's a twist on a top crust. The cracker topping is crunchy and buttery, and works really well with sunny ground cherries.

Topping:

4 ounces buttery crackers such as Ritz

2 tablespoons butter, melted

1 tablespoon sugar

Pastry for single-crust pie

1 Granny Smith or other cooking apple

1½ cups husked, ripe ground cherries (7½ to 8 ounces)

½ cup sugar

2 tablespoons cornstarch

½ teaspoon cinnamon

¼ teaspoon nutmeg

1 tablespoon lemon juice

Heat oven to 375°F. Make the topping: Process crackers in food processor until medium consistency; you may also place them in a plastic bag and bash them with a rolling pin. Place in medium mixing bowl. Drizzle with melted butter; add sugar and mix well. Set aside. Line shallow pie plate (not a deep-dish pie plate) with pastry; flute edges decoratively and set aside.

Peel and core apple, then chop to medium-fine consistency. In large mixing bowl, combine chopped apple, ground cherries, sugar, cornstarch, cinnamon and nutmeg; stir gently to combine. Add lemon juice and stir again. Scrape into prepared crust. Spoon cracker topping evenly over filling. Place pie on a baking sheet (to catch drips); cover pie loosely with foil. Bake for 15 minutes, then remove foil and bake until crumb topping is deep golden brown and filling is bubbly, 20 to 25 minutes longer. Cool on wire rack; best served slightly warm, the day it is made.

 A food processor works best for chopping the apple, and if you used it to crush the crackers, you don't have to rinse it out before chopping the apple.

Ground Cherry Jam (no pectin)

About 3 half-pints

1 quart husked, ripe ground cherries (about 1¼ pounds)

2 cups sugar

¼ cup water

¼ cup freshly squeezed lemon juice

1 cinnamon stick, optional

Please read the notes on no-pectin jam in the Green Gooseberry Jam recipe (pg. 70). Ground cherries have less pectin than green gooseberries, so they require longer cooking, but the basic technique is the same.

In heavy-bottomed non-aluminum 2-quart pot, combine all ingredients. Heat to boiling over high heat, then reduce heat to medium and mash slightly with a potato masher (don't break up the cinnamon stick). Cook fruit at a moderate boil for 30 minutes. Remove jam from the heat to prevent overcooking while you test for doneness. Place a spoonful on a cool plate and place in the freezer for a few minutes; the jam should hold its shape, without weeping around the edges. If the jam is too thin, return to boiling and cook for another few minutes, then re-test; continue as needed until the consistency is correct. Discard cinnamon stick. Pour into sterilized half-pint canning jars; refrigerate for storage, or process for 10 minutes in a water-bath canner (see pg. 171).

Ground Cherry Filling

About ½ cup; easily increased

¾ teaspoon water

¾ teaspoon cornstarch

5½ ounces ground cherries (about 1 heaping cup)

1 tablespoon sugar

¼ teaspoon vanilla extract

In small bowl, blend together water and cornstarch; set aside. Chop ground cherries coarsely by hand or in mini food processor. In small, heavy-bottomed saucepan, combine ground cherries, sugar and vanilla. Heat to boiling over medium-high heat, then cook, stirring frequently, until mixture is no longer runny; this will take 8 to 10 minutes. Add cornstarch mixture, stirring constantly; cook for 1 to 2 minutes longer, or until thick. Cool before using.

Use this to prepare Easy Bear Claws (pg. 20), Fruit-Striped Cookie Fingers (pg. 119), or Fruit-Filled Muffins (pg. 146). Refrigerate extra filling, and use to top oatmeal or toast.

Sweet and Snappy Ground Cherry Salsa   About 1 cup

The fruity, sweet taste of ground cherries makes a wonderful foil to the bite of hot peppers and the tang of fresh cilantro. Enjoy this salsa with chicken fajitas, bean burritos or tostadas, or warm tortilla chips.

1 clove garlic

1 or 2 fresh jalapeño peppers, depending on heat level desired

About ¼ cup fresh cilantro leaves

1 cup husked, ripe ground cherries* (about 5 ounces)

One-quarter of a medium red onion

1 tablespoon seasoned rice vinegar

¼ teaspoon salt, or to taste

Place garlic in food processor and chop until fine. Add pepper(s) and pulse on and off a few times. Add cilantro and process until everything is finely chopped. Transfer mixture to small mixing bowl. Add ground cherries to food processor and chop to medium consistency; the texture doesn't have to be completely even so don't worry if there are a few larger chunks of fruit in the mix. Transfer ground cherries to mixing bowl. Cut onion into ¼-inch dice; add to mixing bowl. Add vinegar and salt. Stir well to mix. Let stand for 15 minutes, then taste for seasoning and adjust salt if necessary. Serve at room temperature; refrigerate leftovers.

*Some sources say that smooth ground cherry (*Physalis longifolia*) should not be eaten raw, so it is best to prepare this with a different species.

 This is a very juicy salsa, so you may want to place a fork rather than a spoon into the serving dish. Use any leftover liquid to add spice to a pot of beans or a stir-fry.

Other recipes in this book featuring ground cherries:
Dehydrated Wild Berries and Fruits, pgs. 168–169

Quick ideas for using ground cherries:
Cut in half and add to fruit salads or green salads (note the comment in the intro text on pg. 78 regarding raw ground cherries).
Add dehydrated ground cherries to oatmeal or other hot cereal, either during or after cooking.

HACKBERRIES *(Celtis occidentalis)*

Hackberry is common in urban areas, yet few people notice its fruit; fewer still realize that the small, dark, berry-like drupe is edible and tasty. A few texts refer to the tree as "sugarberry," and mention that the sweet fruit is used primarily as a trail nibble; several note that Native Americans used dried, crushed sugarberry to season venison.

Hackberries have a large pit, with thin flesh. But the pit is edible, especially with proper preparation, and the fruit is quite sweet, with a date-like flavor.

The flesh is dry but very sweet, with a flavor reminiscent of dates, apples and oranges mixed together. Unfortunately, there is precious little of it; most of the fruit consists of a large pit. Unlike the hard stones in cherries and plums, however, the hackberry pit is edible; it is brittle but soft enough to chew. The sensation is unusual, and trail nibblers usually discard the pit.

Here's a recipe I developed for my book, *Abundantly Wild.*

Pillow Cookies with Hackberry Filling   About 30 cookies

The sweet filling has an unusual texture from the hackberry pits.

Filling:

⅔ **cup hackberry fruits, stems removed**

⅓ **cup sugar**

½ **cup water**

½ **cup chopped pecans or other nuts**

Dough:

½ **cup (1 stick) unsalted butter, softened**

½ **cup (packed) brown sugar**

½ **cup white sugar**

1 **egg**

1 **teaspoon lemon extract, orange extract or vanilla extract**

½ **teaspoon baking soda**

½ **teaspoon salt**

2 **cups all-purpose flour**

First, prepare the filling. Pound hackberries with mortar and pestle until pits are well pulverized; for the least crunchy filling, pound until hackberries are reduced to a smooth paste. (Tip: It's easiest to work in small batches of a tablespoon or two at a time; this way, no large chunks of pit will escape your notice. Scrape pounded fruit into a small saucepan as you go, and continue until all fruit has been pounded.)

Combine pounded fruit with sugar and water in small saucepan. Heat over medium heat, stirring constantly, until boiling gently. Cook for 4 minutes or until thick, stirring constantly. Stir in pecans. Remove from heat and let cool completely before assembling the cookies.

To make dough, cream butter in mixing bowl with electric mixer. Gradually add brown and white sugars, beating until smooth. Add egg, extract, baking soda and salt; beat well. Add flour and beat just until mixed. If you prepare the dough right after cooking the filling, gather the dough into a ball, wrap it tightly and refrigerate until you're ready to bake. Or, simply prepare dough after the filling has cooled, and proceed immediately to baking.

When you're ready to bake, heat oven to 350°F. Lightly spray 2 baking sheets with non-stick spray; set aside. Roll out half of the dough about ⅛ inch thick, or just a bit thicker. Cut into 2-inch circles with a glass or cookie cutter. Place half of the circles on prepared baking sheet, allowing ½ inch between circles. Place 1 teaspoon filling mixture in center of each circle, keeping it away from edges. Place a circle of dough over each mound of filling, forming it into a gentle dome shape over filling and gently pressing the edges together (they will seal together during baking, so don't worry about pressing too hard). Repeat with remaining ingredients to fill the second baking sheet. Bake until golden brown, 13 to 15 minutes. Cool before serving.

Hackberry pits are very crunchy even when crushed fairly fine. It is an odd sensation to encounter in a cookie—not unpleasant, just unexpected, rather like finding a piece of eggshell that accidentally got into the dough. But unlike the eggshell, the pieces of hackberry pit can be chewed and swallowed. The more time you spend pounding the hackberries with the mortar and pestle, the smoother and less crunchy the filling will be.

HAWTHORNS *(Crataegus* spp.)

Numerous varieties of hawthorn grow in our area, and it's hard to know exactly which species you've found. The fruit, usually called a haw, looks like a crabapple, but the seeds in the fruit are larger. Haws of some varieties, or from individual trees, are small, and there is very little flesh in proportion to the seeds. Nevertheless, what flesh and skin there is has a lot of flavor, so these small haws can be used to make juice. If you're lucky, however, you'll find a tree whose fruits are large, soft and fleshy. These haws have enough flesh to make jam; or, the seeds can be removed and the fruit used in pies and other baked goods. The flavor of a good haw is outstanding—rather like a pear with apple and almond overtones.

All hawthorn fruits are edible. The best for cooking have a large amount of fruit in proportion to the seeds; these can be cut up and used like crabapples.

To prepare large haws for use in pies or other recipes that use pieces of fruit rather than pulp, I use a table knife to cut or break them open. My feeling is that if I have to use a sharp knife, either the haw isn't ripe enough, or it is too hard because it's nothing but seeds. Once the haw is open, scrape out the seeds and any blackish tissue surrounding them; if soft, clean flesh adheres to the seeds, scrape it off with the knife before discarding the seed. Pull or cut away the blossom end and the stem, then feel the flesh carefully with your fingertips to be sure there isn't a tooth-shattering seed hidden in the piece. Place the cleaned, seedless haw chunks, and any flesh you've scraped from the seeds, into a measuring cup. Because haws vary so much in size, it's hard to predict the yield; in general, you'll get about ½ cup of cleaned, ready-to-cook haw chunks from a pound of whole, large haws (roughly a quart, give or take).

To prepare hawthorn juice, place whole haws in non-aluminum pot. Add water to generously cover the fruit. Heat to boiling over high heat, then reduce heat and boil gently for 20 minutes, or until the fruit is very soft. Mash as best you can with a potato masher, making sure that each fruit has been opened. Add a little more water if it looks too dry, and cook for 5 minutes longer; the pulpy, seedy mixture should be well covered with water. Transfer the mixture to a strainer lined with doubled, dampened cheesecloth and let it drip for 30 minutes; if you're making jelly, don't squeeze the fruit or the jelly will be cloudy. After the clear liquid has dripped away, set it aside and squeeze the fruit into a different container; you can use this slightly cloudy juice as a beverage or for cooking. Yield varies quite a bit, because hawthorns vary in size; in general, you'll get 1½ cups of pink juice per pound of hawthorns.

Hawthorn and Sausage Brunch Casserole
6 to 8 servings

Hawthorns work really well with the sausage and cheese in this simple dish. It's a natural for brunch, or even a light supper.

8 ounces breakfast-style pork sausage (casings removed if links)

¼ cup diced onion

1¼ cups whole or 2% milk

3 eggs

½ teaspoon dry mustard powder

4 or 5 slices day-old firm white bread (Italian bread works well)

¾ to 1 cup cleaned, seedless hawthorn chunks

1½ cups shredded mozzarella cheese, divided

Heat oven to 375°F. Spray an 8-inch-square baking dish with nonstick spray; set aside. In medium skillet, cook sausage over medium heat, stirring to break up, until no longer pink. Drain off excess grease. Add onion and cook, stirring frequently, until sausage is lightly browned and onion is tender, about 5 minutes. Set aside to cool slightly.

In large mixing bowl, combine milk, eggs and mustard powder; beat well with a fork and set aside. Now, use a blender to make fresh breadcrumbs. Start by tearing bread into 1-inch chunks. Turn the blender on high. Drop chunks from one slice into the blender, immediately re-covering it; the bread pops up very high and can make quite a mess if you don't keep it covered. Process until bread has been chopped into medium-fine crumbs. Transfer breadcrumbs to a large bowl; repeat with remaining bread. Measure 2½ cups of crumbs; if you have extra crumbs, see tip below.

Add measured crumbs, sausage mixture, hawthorn chunks and 1 cup of the cheese to the milk mixture. Stir well, then scrape into prepared dish. Bake, uncovered, for 25 minutes. Sprinkle remaining cheese over the casserole; bake for 5 minutes longer, or until cheese has melted. Remove from oven and let stand 10 minutes before serving.

Substitution: Use crabapple chunks, cored and cut up, in place of the hawthorns.

If you have any breadcrumbs remaining, you can spread them out on a baking sheet and let them dry at room temperature for a few days, stirring occasionally; when completely dry, store in a jar and use in any recipe calling for dry breadcrumbs.

Hawthorn Jelly

3 cups hawthorn juice

Half of a 1.75-ounce box powdered pectin

½ teaspoon butter, optional (helps reduce foaming)

3 cups sugar

Prepare and process as directed in Jelly Instructions (using pectin), pg. 164.

Variation: Use a mix of hawthorn and crabapple juice for a lovely, pinkish Hawthorn-Crabapple Jelly.

Other recipes in this book featuring hawthorns:
Fruits of the Forest Pie, pg. 156
Six Recipes Using Wild Fruit Juice or Syrup, pgs. 158–162
Wild Berry or Fruit Syrup, pg. 163

Quick ideas for using hawthorns:
Use the juice in place of apple juice, for cooking or as a beverage.
Use hawthorn chunks to substitute for chopped apple or pear in recipes for
baked goods. Watch out for the seeds when eating!

HIGHBUSH CRANBERRIES *(Viburnum trilobum)*

Although unrelated to true cranberries (*Vaccinium macrocarpon* and others), highbush cranberry fruits taste remarkably like their namesake. They contain a single flat seed, which is hard and bitter, so they must be processed differently than true cranberries. They also have a foul-tasting lookalike, the guelder rose or European cranberry (*Viburnum opulus*). At a quick glance, it's tough to distinguish between these two plants. The easiest way is to simply taste a ripe fruit. If it tastes like a cranberry with just a slight tang of bitterness, harvest away; if it's a guelder rose, you probably

I've noticed that fruits on highbush cranberry plants often look sparse because they are quickly picked over by birds, while guelder rose plants at the same time are copious with fruit—possibly ignored until the birds have no choice.

won't want to pick any because the fruit is extremely bitter. It's not toxic—although large quantities may cause intestinal problems—so it's safe to sample one.

Highbush cranberries grow in large clusters on the plants, so it's easy to harvest a good quantity. They can be picked when bright red but still hard, or later, when the fruits have softened naturally. If you pick more than you can process, simply pull the fruits off the clusters and freeze them; when thawed, they will be soft and can be processed without cooking. A 1-gallon ice cream pail full of clusters will yield about 2 quarts of cleaned fruits (after the stems have been removed), weighing about 2½ pounds.

Highbush cranberries must be juiced or puréed before using in recipes. Fruits picked when soft, or softened in the freezer, can be processed without cooking; fruits picked when still hard must be stewed first. To stew highbush cranberries, pull off the stems, measure the fruits and place in a non-aluminum pot. For purée, add 1 cup water per quart of stemless fruit; for juice, add 3 cups water per quart of fruit. Heat to boiling, then reduce the heat; cover and simmer for about 5 minutes, gently crushing with a potato masher near the end. If you're working with uncooked fruits which were soft when picked, or have been softened in the freezer, simply combine the fruits with the appropriate amount of water in a clean bucket, and gently crush with a potato masher.

For juice, transfer the prepared fruit to a strainer lined with doubled, dampened cheesecloth and let it drip for 30 minutes; if you're making jelly, don't squeeze the fruit or the jelly will be cloudy. After the clear liquid has dripped away, set it aside and squeeze the fruit into a different container; you can use this slightly cloudy juice as a beverage or for cooking. **For purée,** process the prepared fruit through a food mill, discarding the seeds. A quart of stemmed fruits will yield about 3¼ cups of juice, or about 2 cups of purée.

Highbush cranberries are rich in vitamin C; the purée or juice can be added to other fruits when baking, or sweetened and used on its own. The juice is often used to make delicious jelly; the purée can be used to make jam. In his book, *The Forager's Harvest*, wild foods specialist Sam Thayer writes that juice or purée made from fruits that were picked when soft (or softened in the freezer) and processed without stewing taste better than those made from fruits which have been stewed.

Highbush Cranberry Spice Cake

9 servings

This cake gets its delightful flavor from the highbush cranberries and the spices. The cream cheese frosting is the perfect finish, but a sprinkling of powdered sugar also works well.

6 tablespoons unsalted butter, softened

$2/3$ cup white sugar

$1/2$ cup (packed) golden brown sugar

1 egg

$1\frac{1}{4}$ cups all-purpose flour

$3/4$ teaspoon cinnamon

$3/4$ teaspoon baking powder

$1/2$ teaspoon baking soda

$1/4$ teaspoon ground cloves

$1/8$ teaspoon nutmeg

$2/3$ cup highbush cranberry purée

$1/2$ cup golden raisins

$1/2$ cup chopped walnuts

Heat oven to 350°F. Spray 8-inch-square baking dish with nonstick spray; set aside. In large mixing bowl, beat butter with electric mixer until light. Add white and brown sugars; beat for about 1 minute. Add egg; beat about 1 minute longer.

Place a wire-mesh strainer on a dinner plate. Add flour, cinnamon, baking powder, baking soda, cloves and nutmeg. Shake strainer over the mixing bowl to sift about half of the flour into the butter mixture. Add half of the highbush cranberry purée to the butter mixture; stir well with wooden spoon. Sift remaining flour into mixture; add remaining purée and stir until combined. Stir in raisins and nuts. Scrape into prepared pan, spreading evenly. Bake until a toothpick inserted in the center comes out clean, 35 to 40 minutes. Transfer pan to wire rack and let stand until cool. Frost with cream cheese frosting (recipe follows), or sprinkle with powdered sugar if you prefer.

See companion *Wild Berries & Fruits Field Guide of MN, WI and MI* – page 140

Cream Cheese Frosting

4 tablespoons (half of a stick) butter, softened

4 ounces cream cheese, softened (reduced-fat works fine)

1 teaspoon vanilla extract

1 cup powdered sugar

In large mixing bowl, beat butter, cream cheese and vanilla with electric mixer on high until light and fluffy. Hold a wire-mesh strainer over the bowl and add powdered sugar to strainer. Shake strainer to sift into the butter. Beat until smooth. Refrigerate leftover cake for storage if using cream cheese frosting.

Highbush Sunrise

Bright red highbush cranberry syrup stands in for the grenadine in the classic tequila sunrise ... a delightful difference!

2 ounces gold tequila

4 to 6 ounces top-quality orange juice

1 tablespoon highbush cranberry syrup (pg. 163)

Orange slice and maraschino cherry, for garnish

Fill a tall glass with ice. Add tequila first, then the orange juice. Now pour the syrup into the glass, as close to the side as possible; it should settle to the bottom and then slowly rise to the top. Garnish with orange slice and cherry. (If your syrup isn't thick enough, the sunrise effect may not work ... just stir and enjoy.)

Curried Sweet Potato Soup with HBC Garnish

4 to 6 servings

This is a splendid autumn soup. The highbush cranberry purée makes a lovely, and flavorful, garnish that looks particularly pretty atop the orange soup.

½ cup highbush cranberry purée

2 tablespoons sugar

½ teaspoon finely grated orange zest
  (colored rind only, with none of the white pith)

1 medium onion, diced

1 tablespoon vegetable oil

1 or 2 cloves garlic, minced or pressed

2 teaspoons grated or finely minced fresh gingerroot

1 tablespoon curry powder

2 pounds orange-fleshed sweet potatoes,
  peeled and cut into ¾-inch cubes

½ cup diced roasted red bell peppers
  (from a jar, or make your own)

1 quart chicken broth

¼ teaspoon salt, or to taste

¼ to ½ cup sour cream (reduced-fat works fine)

Prepare the cranberry garnish: In small, heavy-bottomed non-aluminum pan, combine purée, sugar and orange zest. Heat to boiling over medium-high heat, then reduce heat and cook at a very gentle boil for about 10 minutes, stirring frequently. Remove from heat and set aside until needed.

In soup pot, sauté onion in oil over medium heat until beginning to soften, about 5 minutes. Add garlic, gingerroot and curry powder; cook, stirring constantly, until very fragrant, 1 to 2 minutes. Add sweet potatoes, roasted peppers, chicken broth and salt. Heat just to boiling, then reduce heat and cook at a very gentle boil until sweet potatoes are soft, 15 to 20 minutes. Use an immersion blender to purée the soup, or purée in batches in a regular blender (be careful to avoid splashing the hot liquid). Check for seasoning, and adjust salt if necessary. To serve, ladle puréed soup into serving bowls. Spoon some highbush cranberry purée in several dollops on the surface, then use a chopstick to make a swirl pattern by drawing it through the purée in a circular motion. Drop a tablespoon or so of sour cream into the center of each bowl. Serve immediately.

Highbush Cranberry Jelly

5 half-pints

3 cups highbush cranberry juice

Half of a 1.75-ounce box powdered pectin

½ teaspoon butter, optional (helps reduce foaming)

3½ cups sugar

Prepare and process as directed in Jelly Instructions (using pectin), pg. 164.

Highbush Cranberry Jam

About ¾ cup jam per cup of purée

Make as much of this as you wish; since no pectin is needed, you aren't restricted to specific measurements. For a slightly different flavor, use red wine instead of water when stewing the berries (or when mashing berries that you are processing without cooking); Port is particularly delicious.

1 cup highbush cranberry purée

½ cup sugar

**1 teaspoon finely grated orange zest
(colored rind only, with none of the white pith)**

¼ teaspoon ground allspice

¼ teaspoon cinnamon

Pinch of ground nutmeg

Combine all ingredients in heavy-bottomed small saucepan. Heat to boiling, then reduce heat and cook at a very gentle boil, stirring frequently, until mixture is thickened to jam-like consistency. Cooking time is typically 45 minutes to an hour, depending on how loose the purée is. Transfer to sterilized jar(s). Store in refrigerator, or freeze for longer storage.

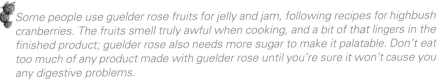

Some people use guelder rose fruits for jelly and jam, following recipes for highbush cranberries. The fruits smell truly awful when cooking, and a bit of that lingers in the finished product; guelder rose also needs more sugar to make it palatable. Don't eat too much of any product made with guelder rose until you're sure it won't cause you any digestive problems.

Highbush-Apple Leather

About 12 ounces finished leather

This fruit leather has a lovely red color and sweet-tart taste from the highbush cranberries. It's a good way to combine two autumn fruits into a useful product that can be kept for a long time.

1½ pounds crabapples, or purchased pie apples such as Granny Smith

1½ cups whole highbush cranberries (about 6 ounces), stems removed before measuring

1¼ cups sugar

1 cup water

Before starting, please read Wild Berry or Fruit Leathers on pg. 170, and prepare your dehydrator or several baking sheets as directed. Wash crabapples. Cut in half, removing stems and blossom ends; if fruit has soft spots or bugs, cut away and discard the affected portions. (If using purchased pie apples, cut into 1-inch chunks, removing stems and blossom ends.) Place in non-aluminum soup pot. Add highbush cranberries, sugar and water. Heat to boiling over high heat. Reduce heat slightly so mixture boils gently and cook, stirring occasionally, for 15 minutes, or until fruit is very tender. Remove from heat and set aside for about 15 minutes; this cools the mixture and also allows the fruit to absorb some of the liquid.

Transfer mixture to a food mill set over a large mixing bowl. Process to remove seeds and apple skins; you should have about 3 cups of thick purée that is the consistency of applesauce. If the purée is runny, transfer it to heavy-bottomed non-aluminum saucepan; boil gently over medium-high heat until mixture thickens, then cool for 15 minutes before proceeding.

Pour the purée onto prepared baking sheets or dehydrator liners. Tilt the sheets to evenly distribute the purée; it should be about ¼ inch deep. Dry at 130°-150°F for about 3 hours, or until the surface feels fairly solid and leathery. Use a spatula to pry up the edge of a piece of the leather, then peel it off and flip it so the underside is exposed. Continue drying until leathery with no sticky spots; total drying time is generally 7 to 8 hours, but this may vary depending on your equipment, the purée and the weather. If you've used baking sheets lined with plastic wrap, the leather can be peeled off any time; if you've used solid liner sheets with a dehydrator, peel off the leather while it is still warm. Roll up all leathers, and wrap in plastic wrap. They keep well at cool room temperature if properly dried; for long-term storage, wrap the plastic-wrapped rolls in freezer paper and store in the freezer.

Highbush Cranberry Sorbet

About 2 pints

Stunning color and tart taste make this sorbet an interesting dessert. Try serving a small scoop of it alongside rich vanilla ice cream, or serve small scoops of several types of sorbet to make a pretty, mixed-color sorbet dessert.

Purée:

2 cups whole highbush cranberries (about 8 ounces), stems removed before measuring

1 cup water

⅓ cup sugar

1½ cups water

1 cup sugar

¼ cup freshly squeezed lemon juice

¼ cup fresh orange juice

Prepare ice cream freezer as directed by manufacturer. In non-aluminum saucepan, combine purée ingredients. Heat to boiling, then reduce heat and simmer for about 10 minutes. Cool slightly, then process through a food mill to remove seeds. Cool purée, then cover with plastic wrap and chill until cold, about 2 hours. Meanwhile, rinse saucepan, then combine the 1½ cups water and 1 cup sugar in cleaned pan. Heat to boiling, stirring constantly; cook until sugar dissolves completely. Remove from heat and set aside to cool.

When purée is cold, combine in large mixing bowl with cooled sugar syrup, lemon juice and orange juice. Pour into ice cream freezer. Churn until mixture is the consistency of soft ice cream. Transfer to an airtight container; cover and freeze at least 3 hours. If sorbet becomes too hard to scoop after a day (or more) in the freezer, place container in refrigerator for 30 minutes prior to serving.

Highbush Peach Relish

This simple-to-prepare relish is fantastic with turkey or ham, and fits right in at holiday time.

**2 cups whole highbush cranberries (about 8 ounces),
stems removed before measuring**

1 ½ cups sugar

½ cup water

¼ teaspoon cinnamon

⅛ teaspoon ground cloves

Pinch of salt

1 tablespoon minced crystallized ginger (found in the spice aisle)

8 ounces frozen sliced peaches, thawed

In non-aluminum saucepan, combine highbush cranberries, sugar, water, cinnamon, cloves and salt; stir well. Heat to boiling; cook for 1 minute, stirring constantly. Reduce heat to simmer and cook for 10 minutes. Cool slightly, then process through a food mill to remove seeds. Stir minced ginger into warm purée. Cut peaches into ½-inch dice, adding to purée as you cut. When all peaches have been added, stir well; set aside until cool. Refrigerate for several hours before serving.

 If you make this relish more than a few days in advance, freeze it until needed, then thaw the day before serving.

Other recipes in this book featuring highbush cranberries:
Wild Berry Vinegar, pg. 13
Six Recipes Using Wild Fruit Juice or Syrup, pgs. 158–162
Wild Berry or Fruit Syrup, pg. 163
As a substitute in Autumn Olive "Berries" for Baking, pg. 8
As a variation in Elderberry Meringue Pie, pg. 66

Quick ideas for using highbush cranberries:
Stir a few tablespoons of the purée into apple, berry or other fruit pie fillings.
Mix 1 part highbush cranberry juice with 2 or 3 parts apple juice;
sweeten to taste.

JUNIPER, COMMON *(Juniperus communis)*

Juniper is a spice plant, with berry-like fruits that are used as seasoning. They have a sharp, clean scent and taste; they are one of the main ingredients used in the traditional distillation of gin, and they have the same smell. They're usually used in marinades or rubs for meat, and are particularly good with strongly flavored meats such as venison and lamb. Some old-world sausages also use juniper as one of the seasoning ingredients.

Pick juniper fruits in late summer or fall, when they are fully developed and blue, with a dusty bloom. Dry them for a few days at room temperature, then store in a tightly sealed spice bottle in a dark cupboard; they'll keep until the next season.

Red Cabbage with Juniper and Bacon   4 servings

This is a hearty dish that goes well with roasted meats or poultry.

¼ pound thick-cut bacon, cut into ½-inch pieces

Half of a small head of red cabbage, cored and cut into 1-inch chunks

Half of a white onion, cut vertically into ¼-inch-wide wedges

¼ cup chicken broth

3 or 4 juniper fruits, crushed

1 tablespoon white wine vinegar

½ teaspoon dried thyme

In large skillet, sauté bacon over medium heat until crisp. Use slotted spoon to transfer to a plate lined with paper towels; discard all but 1 tablespoon of the drippings. Add cabbage and onion to skillet with drippings. Cook over medium heat, stirring occasionally, for about 5 minutes. Add chicken broth, juniper fruits, vinegar and thyme. Cover and cook for 10 minutes, stirring occasionally. Uncover and cook until juices thicken and cabbage is tender, about 5 minutes longer. Sprinkle bacon over cabbage, stirring to combine; cook for a minute or two, until bacon is hot. Serve immediately.

Other recipes in this book featuring juniper fruits:
Venison Roast with Mountain Ash and Juniper Rub, pg. 100
Tart Mountain Ash Jelly, pg. 101

Quick ideas for using juniper fruits:
Use in any recipe calling for purchased juniper berries.
Simmer crushed juniper fruits in melted butter, then use the mixture to baste poultry while it is roasting.

MOUNTAIN ASH *(Sorbus* spp.*)*

Most people who see these lovely, highly decorative trees don't know that the fruits are edible. To be sure, they won't convince anyone who eats one raw, right off the tree; they're quite bitter. But they make an interesting seasoning, and also can be juiced to make an unusual jelly.

Mountain ash are easy to gather in quantity; simply snip off the entire cluster. Wait until they are fully ripe before harvesting. Frost softens the berries and makes them a bit less bitter, so many foragers wait until after the first frost to harvest the fruit. They persist through the winter, and it's fun to trek through the woods on snowshoes to pick mountain ash. Harvested mountain ash fruits keep well in the refrigerator; simply place unwashed clusters—still on the stems—in a plastic bag. Twist the top just lightly, to allow some air to enter the bag, and refrigerate as long as 3 weeks. They also dry well.

Mountain ash trees are a common sight on the rocky shorelines of the Great Lakes, and also grow in cool, moist, sun-dappled woods.

To prepare juice from fresh mountain ash, pull individual fruits off the stems; discard any that are black, or withered and hard. Measure the picked fruit and place in a non-aluminum pot. Add 2 cups of water per 2 cups of picked fruit. Heat to boiling, then reduce the heat; cover and simmer for about 20 minutes. Gently mash the fruit with a potato masher, and cook for 5 minutes longer. Transfer the mixture to a strainer lined with doubled, dampened cheesecloth and let it drip for 30 minutes, pressing lightly to extract more juice. Processed this way, 2 cups of picked fresh fruit will yield about 1 cup juice.

If you're preparing juice from dried mountain ash, follow the same instructions, increasing the water by half (so for 2 cups of dried mountain ash, you'd use 3 cups of water). Increase cooking time from 20 to 30 minutes.

Sweet Mountain Ash Jelly

2 half-pints

1½ cups mountain ash juice

One-third of a 1.75-ounce box powdered pectin

¼ teaspoon butter, optional (helps reduce foaming)

2 cups sugar

Prepare and process as directed in Jelly Instructions (using pectin), pg. 164.

Pork Chops Glazed with Mountain Ash

It's worth it to make a batch of Tart Mountain Ash Jelly (pg. 101) just so you can enjoy these delicious chops. The tangy cranberry-like flavor of the jelly is a perfect complement to seared chops or steaks.

2 boneless pork loin chops, about 1 inch thick

Salt and pepper

1 tablespoon olive oil

½ cup diced onion

3 tablespoons dry sherry

1 cup chicken broth

2 tablespoons Tart Mountain Ash Jelly (pg. 101)

Heat oven to 375°F. Sprinkle chops on both sides with salt and pepper. Heat oil in medium skillet over medium-high heat. Add chops and brown well on both sides. Transfer chops to an oven-proof dish and place in oven to continue cooking while you prepare the sauce in the skillet. If it takes longer than about 10 minutes to make the sauce, remove the dish from the oven and set it aside, covered, until the sauce is ready.

Pour off all but a thin film of oil from skillet. Add onion and cook over medium heat for about 3 minutes, stirring frequently. Add sherry to skillet, stirring to loosen browned bits. Cook until sherry has evaporated almost completely. Add chicken broth and jelly to skillet. Stir to dissolve jelly. Increase heat to high, and cook until liquid has reduced to just a few tablespoons, stirring frequently.

Return chops and any accumulated juices to skillet, turning to coat with pan juices. Cook until heated through and just done.

Variation: Venison Chops or Steaks Glazed with Mountain Ash
Substitute boneless tender venison steaks or chops for the pork; the venison should be 1 inch thick and trimmed of all fat and connective tissue. Use an oven temperature of 300°F rather than 375°F. Proceed as directed, remembering that venison is best when served rare to medium-rare (the lower oven temperature keeps the steaks warm without further cooking while you make the sauce).

Venison Roast with Mountain Ash and Juniper Rub

6 to 8 servings

Venison is a natural partner for mountain ash and juniper berries, both of which are often part of the deer's diet.

Rub:

¼ cup mountain ash berries, crushed

6 juniper berries, crushed

1 teaspoon dried rosemary leaves, crushed

1 teaspoon dried thyme

1 teaspoon paprika

1 teaspoon salt

½ teaspoon freshly ground pepper

2- to 2½-pound venison roast from the hindquarter

2 tablespoons vegetable oil

1 medium onion, diced

1 cup dry red wine

½ cup sour cream

2 tablespoons currant jelly

2 teaspoons all-purpose flour

2 tablespoons cold water

In small bowl, combine all rub ingredients; mix well. Rinse roast, and pat dry with paper towels. Spread rub mixture on all sides of roast, pressing in. Place roast in plastic food-storage bag; seal and refrigerate overnight.

When you're ready to cook, heat oven to 350°F. Heat oil in Dutch oven over medium-high heat until shimmering. Add roast, and brown on all sides, turning as needed; total browning time will be 10 to 15 minutes. Add onion and wine to Dutch oven. Cover and place in oven. Cook, basting occasionally with pan juices, until desired doneness, 20 minutes per pound for rare and up to 30 minutes per pound for medium-well (don't cook it to well-done, or it will be tough and dry). Remove roast from pan; transfer to a serving plate and cover loosely with foil.

Strain pan juices through wire-mesh strainer into a bowl. Return juices to Dutch oven.

Heat to boiling over medium-high heat. Reduce heat and boil gently until liquid is reduced to ¼ cup, 8 to 10 minutes. Stir in sour cream and jelly; cook until jelly melts. In small bowl, stir together flour and water; add to liquid in Dutch oven, stirring constantly. Cook until sauce is smooth and bubbling, 1 to 2 minutes. Serve sauce over sliced roast.

Substitution: Substitute a beef rump roast for the venison. Proceed as directed.

Tart Mountain Ash Jelly
2 half-pints

This tart jelly makes an interesting accompaniment to chops and steaks, especially venison; it's also very good with cheese and crackers.

2 cups fresh mountain ash berries, or 1¾ cups dried

1½ cups water

½ cup red wine vinegar

10 to 12 juniper berries

10 spicebush berries or whole allspice

½ teaspoon Szechuan peppercorns or whole regular peppercorns

One-quarter of a 1.75-ounce box powdered pectin

½ cup sugar

Sterilize 2 half-pint jars, bands and new lids as described on pg. 171. In non-aluminum saucepan, combine mountain ash berries, water, vinegar, juniper berries, spicebush berries and peppercorns. Heat to boiling, then reduce heat and simmer for 20 minutes if using fresh berries; dried berries need to cook for about 30 minutes. Mash berries lightly with a potato masher, and cook for 5 minutes longer. Strain through double thickness of cheesecloth, pressing lightly on berries to extract more juice.

Combine mountain ash juice and pectin in non-aluminum pot that holds at least 3 quarts. Heat to boiling over high heat, stirring frequently. When mixture comes to a full rolling boil that can't be stirred down, add sugar. Cook, stirring constantly, until mixture again comes to a full, foaming boil. Cook for 2 minutes, stirring constantly. Remove from heat, and stir for a minute or two to settle the foam (if there is still foam on top, skim and discard with a clean metal spoon). Pour into prepared jars, leaving ¼ inch headspace; seal with prepared lids and bands. Process in boiling-water bath for 10 minutes.

Other recipes in this book featuring mountain ash:
Dehydrating Wild Berries and Fruits, pgs. 168–169

MULBERRIES *(Morus alba, M. rubra)*

There are two types of mulberries: white and red. Surprisingly, color of the ripe fruit is not the identifying factor. Some white mulberries are, indeed, whitish when ripe, but more commonly they are pink, red or deep purple; red mulberries are blackish when ripe. Both can be eaten raw or cooked; however, be sure that the fruit you pick is completely ripe and soft, as unripe fruit is not only hard and unpleasant but is also mildly toxic (as are the leaves and all other parts of the plant).

The hardest part about picking mulberries is reaching the fruit, which is usually high up in the tree. The best way to harvest them is to spread a tarp under the tree, then jostle the branches with a stick; ripe fruit will fall onto the tarp and can be gathered. A short, soft stemlet remains attached to the fruit; this should be removed before eating or cooking the fruit. It's easiest to just pinch it off with your fingernails as you're washing the fruit.

Mulberries are very common in urban areas, yet few people seem to pick them for eating. It's too bad, because the fruits are sweet and delicious—and if more folks were interested in picking them, there would be fewer mulberries staining the sidewalks!

To prepare pulp or juice, measure the fruit and place in a non-aluminum pot. For pulp, add ½ cup water per quart of fruit; for juice, add 1 cup water per quart of fruit. Thoroughly crush the fruit with a potato masher to start the juices flowing. Heat to boiling, then reduce the heat; cover and simmer for about 20 minutes. **For pulp,** the mixture is ready to use; you can also purée it in a food processor to make it smoother if you like. **For juice,** transfer the mixture to a strainer lined with doubled, dampened cheesecloth and let it drip for 30 minutes; if you're making jelly, don't squeeze the fruit or the jelly will be cloudy. After the clear liquid has dripped away, set it aside and squeeze the fruit into a different container; you can use this slightly cloudy juice as a beverage or for cooking, and add the leftover, squeezed fruit to applesauce, pie filling or other cooked fruits. Processed this way, a quart of fruit will yield about 1½ cups of pulp, or about 2 cups juice.

Once you've harvested mulberries, use them within a day or two, as they will spoil quickly. They freeze beautifully; simply pack them into containers or heavyweight plastic bags and freeze. They can be dried successfully; the texture of a dried mulberry is similar to that of a dried fig. Dried mulberries can be eaten out of hand as a nibble, or rehydrated in warm water and used like fresh berries.

Mulberry Thumbprint Cookies

About 28 cookies

Whole mulberries nestle inside a thumbprint pressed into a rich, buttery cookie.

- ½ cup (1 stick) unsalted butter, softened
- ¼ cup confectioner's sugar, plus additional for garnish
- 1½ teaspoons vanilla extract
- 1 cup all-purpose flour
- ¼ teaspoon salt
- ¼ cup very finely chopped pecans
- ¾ cup (approximate) fresh mulberries

In mixing bowl, combine butter, ¼ cup confectioner's sugar and the vanilla. Beat with electric mixer until light and fluffy, about 2 minutes; scrape bowl several times. Place a wire-mesh strainer over the mixing bowl; add flour and salt, then shake strainer to sift flour into the butter mixture. Add nuts. Stir with spatula or wooden spoon until well-mixed. Cover and refrigerate for an hour (or longer); this makes the dough easy to handle.

When ready to bake, heat oven to 350°F. Roll chilled dough into balls that are about 1 inch in size. Place on ungreased baking sheet, about 1½ inches apart. Use your thumb to press a large indentation into the center of each ball. Place 3 or 4 mulberries (depending on size) into each indentation. Bake for 18 to 23 minutes, or until cookies are just set and are lightly golden brown. Remove baking sheet(s) from oven; use the back of a spoon to gently press each group of berries into the dough. Put a little confectioners' sugar into a wire-mesh strainer and shake it gently over the cookies to dust them lightly. Transfer to wire rack. Cool before serving.

Mulberry Jelly

4 half-pints

- 2¾ cups mulberry juice
- 2 tablespoons lemon juice
- Two-thirds of a 1.75-ounce box powdered pectin
- ½ teaspoon butter, optional (helps reduce foaming)
- 3½ cups sugar

Prepare and process as directed in Jelly Instructions (using pectin), pg. 164.

Mulberry Ripple Cheesecake 1 cheesecake (10 to 12 servings)

This cheesecake is a great dessert for a large dinner party, and also works to take along to a potluck because it serves up to 12 people.

Crust:

¾ cup graham cracker crumbs

½ cup ground pecans

2 tablespoons white sugar

2 tablespoons (packed) golden brown sugar

4 tablespoons (half of a stick) butter, melted

Filling:

¾ cup smooth mulberry pulp (processed in blender)

2 tablespoons white sugar

1 teaspoon cornstarch

3 packages cream cheese (8 ounces each), softened

1 can (14 ounces) sweetened condensed milk

¼ cup freshly squeezed lemon juice

1 teaspoon vanilla extract

3 eggs, at room temperature

Heat oven to 350°F. Spray 9-inch springform pan (with removable edge) with nonstick spray. In mixing bowl, combine graham cracker crumbs, pecans, white sugar and brown sugar; stir to mix well. Drizzle butter over while stirring; continue stirring until well mixed. Pour into prepared pan; use a small glass to firmly press the crumbs evenly into the pan and about 1 inch up the sides. Bake until light golden brown, 10 to 12 minutes. Transfer to a wire rack; let cool while you prepare the filling. Reduce oven to 300°F.

For the filling: Combine mulberry pulp and sugar in small saucepan. Heat over medium heat, stirring constantly, until sugar dissolves, about 3 minutes. Stir in cornstarch. Increase heat to medium-high and cook, stirring frequently, until mixture thickens, about 1 minute. Remove from heat and cool slightly, then pour into a measuring cup that has a spout and place in freezer to chill for a few minutes.

In large mixing bowl, beat cream cheese with electric mixer until light and fluffy, about 2 minutes. Gradually add condensed milk, beating constantly and scraping the sides of the bowl as necessary. Add lemon juice and vanilla; beat until well mixed. Add eggs, one at a time, beating well after each addition.

Pour cream cheese mixture into crust, spreading evenly. Drizzle the mulberry mixture over the top, pouring in several thin circles to form a bull's-eye pattern. Swirl a table knife through the circles to create a ripple effect; don't let the knife go all the way down to the crust. Bake until cheesecake is puffy around the edges but still a bit loose in the center, 50 to 60 minutes. Transfer to a wire rack; set aside to cool completely. Wrap tightly with plastic wrap or foil, and refrigerate at least 8 hours or overnight.

To serve, run a sharp knife around the edge of the pan to loosen the cake, then carefully remove the ring around the edge. Cut into thin slices; if the knife is sticking, dip it into hot water and dry quickly before continuing.

Variation: Substitute 1 cup raspberry or blackberry purée for the mulberry pulp; increase cornstarch to 1½ teaspoons. Because this purée is a bit thinner than the mulberry pulp, it needs a bit more cooking time to reduce it before adding the cornstarch.

Note that the cheesecake must be prepared at least a half-day in advance; overnight is better, to give the cheesecake time to firm and allow the flavors to meld.

Mulberry Filling

About ½ cup; easily increased

½ teaspoon water

½ teaspoon cornstarch

5 ounces mulberries (about 1 cup)

1 tablespoon grated apple

2 teaspoons sugar

1½ teaspoons lemon juice

In small bowl, blend together water and cornstarch; set aside. In small, heavy-bottomed saucepan, combine mulberries, apple, sugar and lemon juice. Crush fruit gently with a potato masher to start juices flowing. Heat to boiling over medium-high heat, then cook, stirring frequently, until mixture is no longer runny; this will take 10 to 12 minutes. Add cornstarch mixture, stirring constantly; cook for about 1 minute longer, or until thick. Cool before using.

Use this to prepare Easy Bear Claws (pg. 20), Fruit-Striped Cookie Fingers (pg. 119), or Fruit-Filled Muffins (pg. 146). Refrigerate extra filling, and use to top oatmeal or toast.

Mulberry-Rhubarb Pie with Crumble Topping

1 pie (6 to 8 servings)

Rhubarb adds a nice touch of tartness and complexity to the mulberries, which are quite sweet on their own. It's also in season when mulberries are ripe, making this a perfect combination.

Crumble topping:

4 tablespoons (half of a stick) cold unsalted butter

⅔ cup all-purpose flour

¼ cup (packed) light brown sugar

3 tablespoons white sugar

¼ teaspoon cinnamon

A pinch of salt

Ready-to-use pastry for single-crust pie

¾ cup sugar

3 tablespoons quick-cooking tapioca

2 cups fresh rhubarb, cut into ½-inch chunks before measuring

1½ cups fresh mulberries

2 tablespoons unsalted butter, cut into bits

½ teaspoon vanilla extract

Heat oven to 400°F. Prepare crumble topping: Cut butter into ½-inch cubes and combine in food processor with remaining topping ingredients. Pulse for a few short bursts, just until mixture resembles coarse meal. Transfer to a bowl and refrigerate until needed; don't wash the food processor, as you'll need it in the next step.

Fit pastry into pie plate, then turn under and crimp edges; set aside. In food processor, combine sugar and tapioca; process for 15 seconds (this makes the tapioca finer, so it cooks more evenly). Pour into large mixing bowl. Add rhubarb, mulberries, butter and vanilla; stir gently. Spoon evenly into crust. Use a spoon to sprinkle crumble topping evenly over filling. Place pie on a baking sheet (to catch drips) and bake in the lower third of the oven for 30 minutes. Reduce heat to 350°F, and bake for 30 minutes longer, until topping is nicely browned and filling is bubbly. Cool on a rack for 2 hours before serving.

Rice Pudding with Wild Berries

Tender, custardy rice pudding is studded with colorful fruits.

1 tablespoon butter, softened

2¾ cups whole milk

6 egg yolks

¾ cup sugar

½ teaspoon vanilla extract

½ teaspoon lemon extract

1 teaspoon cinnamon

⅛ teaspoon salt

4 cups cooked long-grain rice (from about 1½ cups raw rice)

1 cup mulberries, raspberries or blackberries, cut in half if long

Heat oven to 350°F. Generously butter 9-inch-square baking dish; set aside. In saucepan, heat milk over medium heat until small bubbles appear around the edges; remove from heat. In large mixing bowl, use a whisk to beat egg yolks and sugar until light. Add warm milk, vanilla and lemon extracts, cinnamon and salt; whisk to blend. Add rice and stir with a wooden spoon until well mixed. Add mulberries; stir gently to mix. Scrape mixture into prepared dish. Bake until lightly browned on top, 40 to 50 minutes. Cool for 5 to 10 minutes, and serve while still warm.

Other recipes in this book featuring mulberries:
Six Recipes Using Wild Fruit Juice or Syrup, pgs. 158–162
Wild Berry or Fruit Syrup, pg. 163
Dehydrating Wild Berries and Fruits, pgs. 168–169

Quick ideas for using mulberries:
Mix a few into any baking recipe that uses raspberries. The mulberries have a more solid texture and are generally a bit larger than raspberries, so they should be cut into two shorter halves if longer than ¾ inch to make them more similar to the raspberries.

NANNYBERRIES, WITHE-ROD and BLACKHAWS
(Viburnum lentago, V. cassinoides, and V. prunifolium)

These three *Viburnum* species are very similar in appearance and eating quality; they can be handled in the same way in the kitchen. All make excellent trail nibbles when fully ripe and soft; even when the fruits dry and shrivel later in the season, they are still tasty, with a flavor that is somewhat like a prune with tropical overtones. Withe-rod is sometimes called "wild raisin" because in its dried, wrinkled state, it resembles the common domestic fruit.

It's best to pick these fruits when they are ripe and plump, before they dry and shrivel. They're still edible in the dried state, and make a delicious snack; but if you're making purée, your yield will be poor if you work with dried fruits.

Withe-rod is blue-black when ripe, while nannyberry and blackhaw are a deeper black. Fruits of all three grow in flat-topped clusters; when you find a plant with ripe fruit, it's easy to harvest a good quantity by snipping off the entire cluster. If there are a few underripe fruits on the cluster, leave them out at room temperature for a few days, where they'll ripen completely; the ripe fruits on the cluster will be fine while the others ripen, so you don't need to separate them. Store ripe fruits in the refrigerator, where they'll keep for several weeks.

All three fruits are excellent raw, eaten out-of-hand as a snack, although the large, flat seed is inedible and must be spit out (think of it like watermelon; the seeds are similar). The fruits also make an outstanding purée. Pick the fruits off the stems, then measure them and place in a heavy-bottomed, non-aluminum pot. Add 3 cups water per quart of picked fruit. Heat to boiling, then reduce heat and simmer gently, uncovered, for about 45 minutes. Process through a food mill while still warm, then discard the seeds. A quart of ripe, but not dry, fruit produces 2 to 3 cups of thick, luscious purée; yield will be considerably less if the fruit is dry when processed.

If you prefer a thinner product, similar to apricot nectar, reduce simmering time to 20 minutes; cover the pan during simmering. Process through the food mill (or a conical strainer). Scrape the pulpy seed mixture remaining in the food mill back into the cooking pot, and add about ¾ cup water; stir well to loosen the pulp. Return mixture to the food mill and process again, combining the two batches of resulting purée. You should get 3 to 4 cups of nectar.

Purées of nannyberry, withe-rod and blackhaw make an excellent, jam-like spread with no further processing (other than some additional sweetening if you like); they're rather like apple butter. They can also be used for baking, sauces and other delicious dishes. The recipes on the following pages call for nannyberry purée or nectar, but purée and nectar made from withe-rod or blackhaw may be substituted in equal amounts, with great results.

Nannyberry Barbecue Sauce

1 cup

This easy sauce gets a rich, sweet taste from the nannyberries.

¾ cup nannyberry purée

2 tablespoons honey

1½ tablespoons Dijon mustard

2 teaspoons lemon juice

1½ teaspoons crumbled, dried thyme

½ teaspoon salt, or to taste

¼ teaspoon freshly ground black pepper, or to taste

In small mixing bowl, combine all ingredients; stir well and refrigerate until needed. This will keep for a month in the refrigerator.

 Use this with pork or chicken, as you would regular barbecue sauce. See below for a simple grilled pork chop recipe as an example.

Pork Loin Chops with Nannyberry Barbecue Sauce

4 servings

Putting the sauce on the chops after they're turned prevents it from burning.

4 boneless pork loin chops (about 6 ounces each)

Salt and pepper

2 to 3 tablespoons Nannyberry Barbecue Sauce

Prepare grill for direct, medium heat (see "Grilling: Direct vs. Indirect Heat," pg. 151). Season chops lightly on both sides with salt and pepper. Place on grate directly over heat; cover and cook for about 3 minutes, until nicely marked. Rotate chops 90 degrees, keeping the same side down; re-cover and cook for about 2 minutes longer. Turn chops. Spoon a generous amount of sauce over each chop. Re-cover grill and cook until chops are cooked through, 3 to 8 minutes depending on thickness of chops.

Nannyberry Carrot Cake

12 servings

Nannyberry nectar gives a rich, deep color and delightful sweetness to this cake. It's great just as it is, but if you like, you can top it with Cream Cheese Frosting (pg. 91) or serve it with lightly sweetened whipped cream.

2 cups all-purpose flour

1 teaspoon baking soda

¾ teaspoon cinnamon

½ teaspoon salt

3 eggs

1⅓ cups sugar

½ cup vegetable oil

¾ cup nannyberry nectar

1 teaspoon vanilla extract

2¼ cups grated raw carrots

1 cup chopped walnuts, hickory nuts or pecans

Heat oven to 350°F. Grease and flour 9x13-inch baking dish; set aside. Sift together flour, baking soda, cinnamon and salt. In mixing bowl, combine eggs, sugar, oil, nannyberry nectar and vanilla. Beat with electric mixer until smooth. Add flour mixture; stir with a wooden spoon just until combined. Add carrots and nuts; stir just until combined. Scrape into prepared dish. Bake until a toothpick inserted in the center comes out clean, 40 to 50 minutes. Serve warm or at room temperature.

Nannyberry Filling

⅓ cup nannyberry purée

2 tablespoons golden raisins

2 tablespoons (packed) brown sugar

**½ teaspoon grated orange zest
(colored rind only, not the white pith), optional**

Combine all ingredients in small bowl; mix well.

Use this to prepare Easy Bear Claws (pg. 20), Fruit-Striped Cookie Fingers (pg. 119), or Fruit-Filled Muffins (pg. 146). Refrigerate extra filling, and use to top oatmeal or toast.

Other recipes in this book featuring nannyberries, withe-rod and blackhaws:
As a substitute in Autumn Olive "Berries" for Baking, pg. 8

Quick ideas for using nannyberries, withe-rod and blackhaws:
Sweeten a batch of nectar, prepared as directed on pg. 108, to taste; chill and serve as a delicious breakfast drink.
Add a handful of whole fruits to cut-up apples when making applesauce; note that this works only with recipes that call for cooking and then straining the apples to remove the seeds.
Sweeten the purée a bit, and serve on top of hot oatmeal.

AMERICAN WILD PLUM (*Prunus americana*)

Wild plums are easy to identify; they look a lot like the ones you buy in the store, but smaller. American wild plums are typically bright reddish-orange when ripe. Beach plums (*P. maritima*) were planted years ago in a few locations alongside Lake Michigan, and it is possible that survivors of those plants may be found; beach plum fruits are reddish-purple to reddish-black. Canadian plums (*P. nigra*) are found occasionally in our area; ripe fruits are yellowish to reddish. Eating quality of all wild plums varies between species and also from tree to tree; some are too tart to eat raw and are best used for cooked dishes. Others are sweet and juicy, begging to be popped into the mouth and savored on the spot.

Note that plums don't ripen well off the tree, so it's best to harvest only ripe plums, which will be slightly soft. Unripe plums can cause digestive upset.

Plums can be cut from the pit for use in recipes; they are also used to make purée or, less commonly, juice. Unlike many wild fruits, cut-up plums work well in savory dishes as well as sweet ones. I've never encountered a wild plum whose flesh separated easily and cleanly from the pit; unlike some domestic plums, wild plums cling tightly to the pit. Use a paring knife to cut the flesh away, cutting as close to the pit as you can. Plum skin is a bit sour, but I generally leave the skin on the fruit when I'm pitting. If you wish to remove the skins, drop a few whole plums into a pan of boiling water, then boil until the skin splits slightly; this takes about a minute. Immediately transfer the plums to a bowl filled with ice water. You can now peel the skins off, then cut the flesh away from the pit and proceed with your recipe.

To prepare purée or juice, it's not necessary to remove the pits; simply cut the plums into rough halves, cutting alongside the pit, and place in a non-aluminum saucepan or pot. For purée, add enough water to come about one-quarter of the way up the plums; for juice, add enough to come about halfway up. Heat to boiling over high heat, then reduce heat and simmer, stirring occasionally, for 10 minutes, or until the plums are very soft.* **For purée,** transfer the cooked fruit mixture to a food mill and process until the pits are largely scraped clean; remove pits individually, then process the mixture remaining in the food mill until all that's left in the food mill is skins. **For juice,** transfer the cooked fruit mixture to a strainer lined with doubled, dampened cheesecloth and let it drip for 30 minutes; if you're making jelly, don't squeeze the fruit or the jelly will be cloudy. After the clear liquid has dripped away, set it aside and squeeze the fruit into a different container; you can use this slightly cloudy juice as a beverage or for cooking.

Yield varies quite a bit with plums; some are very fleshy and produce a good quantity of cut-up fruit or purée, while others are thin-fleshed, yielding much less. If you've found nicely fleshy wild plums, you'll probably get a cup of cut-up chunks (uncooked) per dozen fruits; a pound of fleshy plums typically produces ½ to ¾ cup of cooked purée, or 1½ cups of juice.

*Don't crush the pits during cooking or straining. Plum pits contain small amounts of a cyanide-forming compound that can cause illness if eaten in large quantities.

Asian-Inspired Plum Sauce

About 1¼ cups

This lovely, jewel-like sauce packs a punch from the hot pepper and gingerroot.

2 cloves garlic

1-inch chunk of peeled fresh gingerroot

1 small hot red pepper, seeds and stem removed

Half of a small white onion, cut into 1-inch pieces

Half of a red bell pepper, cored and cut into 1-inch chunks

2 cups cut-up plums, pitted and cut into ½-inch chunks before measuring

⅓ cup brown sugar

⅓ cup seasoned rice vinegar

¼ cup orange juice

½ teaspoon ground coriander

½ teaspoon salt

In food processor, chop garlic, gingerroot and hot pepper until very fine. Add onion and bell pepper; pulse a few times to chop. Add plums; pulse until everything is chopped to medium texture. Transfer mixture to medium, heavy-bottomed non-aluminum saucepan; add remaining ingredients. Heat to boiling over medium-high heat; reduce heat and simmer, stirring frequently, until thick, about 30 minutes. Transfer to clean jars; cool completely. Store in refrigerator.

Serve this with egg rolls or chicken wings, or add it to stir-fries. It's also great when brushed over ribs, pork chops or chicken just before taking them from the grill.

Plum-Dandy Oatmeal Squares

These tasty squares hold up well in a lunchbox.

1½ cups cut-up plums, pitted and cut into ½-inch chunks before measuring

3 tablespoons apple juice, other juice or water

1 tablespoon honey

1½ cups all-purpose flour

½ cup old-fashioned rolled oats

1½ cups (packed) golden brown sugar

¼ teaspoon baking soda

A pinch of salt

⅓ cup vegetable oil

3 tablespoons frozen orange juice concentrate

2 tablespoons cold butter, cut into several chunks

In small saucepan, combine plums, apple juice and honey. Heat to boiling over medium-high heat, then reduce heat so mixture is simmering. Cook, stirring frequently, until plums break up and mixture thickens, about 10 minutes. Remove from heat; set aside until cool.

Heat oven to 350°F. Spray 8-inch-square baking dish with nonstick spray; set aside. In mixing bowl, combine flour, rolled oats, brown sugar, baking soda and salt; mix well with a wooden spoon. Remove ½ cup of the flour mixture, transferring to a small bowl; set aside. Add oil and orange juice concentrate to flour remaining in mixing bowl; stir with wooden spoon until well-mixed and crumbly. Pat flour mixture into prepared baking dish, pressing firmly. Spoon cooled plum filling over crust, spreading evenly; set aside.

Add cold butter to the ½ cup flour mixture in the small bowl. Rub together with your fingertips until the mixture is crumbly. Sprinkle topping over plum filling. Bake until golden brown, about 30 minutes. Cool on wire rack before cutting into squares.

Plum Butter

Plum butter is easy to make in almost any quantity, because it needs no added pectin (and therefore does not require precise measurements). It's fabulous as a spread for toast, or used to top pancakes, waffles or hot cereal.

Wild plums

Water

Sugar

Optional: Cinnamon, cardamom, nutmeg (any or all, as you prefer)

Cut the flesh away from the pits, adding the pitted fruit to a saucepan as you go. (Don't try to make plum butter with fewer than 12 plums; the amount of the cooking purée will be so small that it will burn.) Add cold water to cover the plum pieces. Heat to boiling over medium-high heat, and boil until skins are tender, about 10 minutes. Cool slightly, then strain through a food mill or conical strainer; you could also strain the plums through a wire-mesh strainer, stirring and pushing the fruit through with a wooden spoon.

Measure the strained pulp and transfer to a heavy-bottomed non-aluminum saucepan. Sterilize enough half-pint canning jars, bands and new lids (see pg. 171) to hold the finished plum butter (as a guideline, you'd need 4 half-pint jars for 3 cups of strained pulp). Heat to boiling over medium-high heat, then add ½ to ⅞ cup of sugar per cup of strained plums (the amount depends on the sweetness of the plums and your personal preference), stirring until the sugar dissolves. If using spices, add them now; try ¼ teaspoon of cinnamon or cardamom (or both) per cup of strained pulp, and/or a healthy pinch of nutmeg. Adjust heat so the mixture is boiling, but not so vigorously that the bubbles explode. Cook, stirring frequently, until the mixture is very thick; this will take 15 to 30 minutes, depending on how runny the strained pulp was. Transfer to prepared canning jars. Process in a water-bath canner for 10 minutes, or refrigerate.

Wild Plum Jelly

2¾ cups wild plum juice

Half of a 1.75-ounce box powdered pectin

½ teaspoon butter, optional (helps reduce foaming)

3¼ cups sugar

Prepare and process as directed in Jelly Instructions (using pectin), pg. 164.

Ham Slice with Piquant Plum Sauce

4 servings

A savory plum sauce adds a sweet-and-tangy note to ham in this easy weeknight supper.

¼ cup minced shallots

1 tablespoon butter

1½ cups cut-up plums, pitted and cut into ½ to ¾-inch chunks before measuring

⅓ cup dry sherry

2 tablespoons maple syrup

1 tablespoon coarse (prepared) mustard

¼ teaspoon chili powder blend

1 bone-in ham slice, about 1¼ pounds

Heat oven to 400°F. In saucepan, cook shallots in butter over medium heat, stirring frequently, for 5 minutes. Add plums; cook, stirring frequently, for 5 minutes. Add sherry, maple syrup, mustard and chili powder; stir well. Cook, stirring occasionally, for about 5 minutes, or until plums have softened but still retain their shape. Remove from heat.

Place ham in a baking dish large enough to hold it. Spoon about ⅓ cup of the plum sauce over the ham, spreading evenly. Bake for 10 minutes, or until ham is hot all the way through and sauce is starting to glaze. If you like, turn the broiler on and broil for a minute or so to caramelize the glaze. Cut ham into 4 portions; serve with remaining sauce.

Variation: This recipe would also work with smoked pork chops.

Plum Filling

This filling is really pretty, and adds wonderful jewel tones to baked goods.

1 cup cut-up plums, pitted and cut into ¼-inch chunks before measuring

2 tablespoons sugar

1 tablespoon grated apple

1 teaspoon lemon juice

In small, heavy-bottomed saucepan, combine all ingredients. Crush fruit gently with a potato masher to start juices flowing. Heat to boiling over medium-high heat. Reduce heat; cover and simmer, stirring occasionally, until fruit is tender, 5 to 8 minutes. Mash again. Increase heat to medium-high, and boil, stirring frequently, until thick, about 5 minutes. Cool before using.

Use this to prepare Easy Bear Claws (pg. 20), Fruit-Striped Cookie Fingers (pg. 119), or Fruit-Filled Muffins (pg. 146). Refrigerate extra filling, and use to top oatmeal or toast.

Other recipes in this book featuring wild plums:

Spicy Plum Chutney, pg. 141
Six Recipes Using Wild Fruit Juice or Syrup, pgs. 158–162
Wild Berry or Fruit Syrup, pg. 163
Dehydrating Wild Berries and Fruits, pgs. 168–169

Quick ideas for using wild plums:

Use cut-up wild plums in any recipe that calls for domestic plums; you may need to increase the sugar slightly if your plums are tart.
Sweeten plum purée to taste, then use it to make a delicious fruit leather (see pg. 170 for information on making leathers).
Plum juice makes a wonderful breakfast drink when sweetened to taste. If you're making juice to drink rather than to make jelly, don't worry about making clear juice; squeeze the cheesecloth-wrapped fruit to get more juice. The juice will be thicker than that used to make jelly, and the extra body is nice in juice for drinking.

RED RASPBERRIES, BLACK RASPBERRIES and DEWBERRIES *(Rubus idaeus, R. occidentalis, R. pubescens)*

Red raspberries are one of the most commonly foraged wild fruits; they're easy to identify, abundant and delicious. Black raspberries are less well known, but some foragers (including me) think that they surpass red raspberries in taste. The dewberry family is quite large, and ripe fruits range from red to purple to black; *Rubus pubescens*, listed above, is a red dewberry that is also called dwarf raspberry. Dewberries are locally common, but not as widespread as the two raspberry species.

Raspberries, whether red or black, are delicious both raw and cooked; some dewberries are a bit sour and are better used for jam, jelly, pastries or other cooked dishes.

All of the fruits mentioned here are compound drupes, with lots of small seeds. They're noticeable, but not nearly as bothersome as blackberry seeds; however, some cooks prefer to strain them out when making jam or purée. I seldom bother with this extra step, preferring to enjoy the fruit in its natural state.

To prepare purée or juice, measure the fruit and place in a non-aluminum pot. For purée, add ½ cup water per quart of fruit; for juice, add 1 cup water per quart of fruit. Gently crush the fruit with a potato masher to start the juices flowing. Heat to boiling, then reduce the heat; cover and simmer for about 10 minutes. **For seedless purée,** process the cooked fruit through a food mill, then discard the seeds; if you don't mind the seeds, the purée is ready after cooking. **For juice,** transfer the mixture to a strainer lined with doubled, dampened cheesecloth and let it drip for 30 minutes; if you're making jelly, don't squeeze the fruit or the jelly will be cloudy. After the clear liquid has dripped away, set it aside and squeeze the fruit into a different container; you can use this slightly cloudy juice as a beverage or for cooking, and add the leftover, squeezed fruit to applesauce, pie filling or other cooked fruits. Processed this way, a quart of red raspberries will yield about 1-½ cups of purée, or about 2 cups juice; the yield will be slightly less for black raspberries or dewberries.

To avoid cumbersome ingredients lists, most of the recipes on the following pages simply call for raspberries. You may use red or black raspberries for any of them with no adjustments; if you use dewberries, you may wish to increase the sugar slightly, depending on the sweetness of the berries you've picked.

Fruit-Striped Cookie Fingers

A buttery, rich cookie base is topped with fruit filling in these attractive cookies.

1³/₄ cups all-purpose flour, plus additional for rolling dough

¼ cup powdered sugar

⅛ teaspoon salt

½ cup (1 stick) cold butter, cut into small pieces

4 ounces cream cheese, cut into 1-inch chunks

1 egg yolk

1 tablespoon orange juice

1 teaspoon vanilla extract

½ cup Raspberry Filling (pg. 121), or other wild fruit filling (see "Filling options" below)

In food processor, combine 1¾ cups flour, the powdered sugar and salt; pulse a few times to mix. Add butter and cream cheese; pulse until mixture is coarse and crumbly. In a small bowl, stir together the egg yolk, orange juice and vanilla. Add to flour mixture; pulse a few times, until mixture just begins to come together (do not over-process, or the cookies will be tough). Transfer dough to a gallon-sized plastic food storage bag. Press with your hands (from the outside of the bag) until dough comes together. Flatten dough into a disk; refrigerate at least 1 hour, or as long as 1 day.

When ready to bake, heat oven to 375°F. Divide dough into 2 parts; refrigerate one while you roll out the other. On lightly floured worksurface, roll dough about ¼ inch thick, keeping the rolled-out dough as square as possible. Trim one edge in a straight line, then use a small ruler to mark 1-inch divisions. Cut the dough into 1-inch-wide strips, cutting on the marks. Lay a chopstick in the center of one strip, and press it down into the dough, rolling it back and forth slightly to make a U-shaped channel about ½ inch wide in the center of the strip. Transfer the strip to an ungreased baking sheet. Repeat with remaining strips, keeping them ½ inch apart on the baking sheet.

Spoon filling mixture along the channels, mounding it slightly. Bake until golden brown and firm, 23 to 26 minutes. Remove baking sheets from oven, and immediately use a small knife to cut each strip into 1-inch pieces. Transfer to a wire rack to cool completely. Store at room temperature for up to 5 days; refrigerate or freeze for longer storage.

Filling options: This recipe works with any of the following fillings: Blackberry (pg. 14), Blueberry (pg. 23), Crabapple (pg. 45), Green Gooseberry (pg. 71), Ground Cherry (pg. 82), Mulberry (pg. 105), Nannyberry (pg. 111), Plum (pg. 117), Raspberry (pg. 121), Serviceberry (pg. 136), Strawberry (pg. 145), or Thimbleberry (pg. 154).

Chicken with Wild Raspberry Sauce

4 servings

Wild raspberries make a brightly flavored sauce for this roasted chicken. Serve with steamed rice to capture all the delicious juices.

2 whole bone-in, skin-on chicken breasts, split (4 half-breasts)

½ teaspoon coarse salt such as kosher salt

¼ teaspoon dry mustard powder

A few grinds of black pepper

A dash of nutmeg

1 tablespoon olive oil

1 quart reduced-sodium chicken broth

3 cloves garlic

A few sprigs fresh parsley

1 tablespoon cornstarch, dissolved in 1 tablespoon cold water

1¼ cups raspberries (about 6¼ ounces)

2 teaspoons minced fresh oregano or marjoram

Heat oven to 375°F. Rinse chicken breast halves; pat dry with paper towels. In a small bowl, stir together salt, mustard powder, pepper and nutmeg; rub into chicken on both sides. In large, oven-safe skillet, heat oil over medium-high heat until shimmering. Add chicken breast halves, skin-side down. Cook until nicely browned, about 5 minutes. Use tongs to turn the chicken skin-side up. Transfer skillet to oven; roast until chicken is just cooked through, 15 to 20 minutes (an instant-read thermometer should read 165°F when stuck in the thickest part of the meat).

While chicken is roasting, start preparing the sauce: Combine chicken broth, garlic and parsley in wide saucepan. Heat to boiling over high heat, then cook until liquid has reduced to about 1 cup (see "Reducing Liquid" on pg. 121); it should be ready by the time the chicken breasts are done. Discard parsley; use a fork to mash garlic cloves into the reduced broth.

When chicken is done, remove skillet from oven. Transfer chicken to a serving plate; cover loosely with foil and set aside. Place skillet over medium-high heat. Add reduced broth; cook for about 5 minutes over medium-high heat, stirring frequently. Add cornstarch mixture; cook until sauce thickens and bubbles, 2 to 3 minutes. Add raspberries and oregano. Cook for about 1 minute, stirring frequently. Transfer raspberry sauce to a serving bowl. Serve chicken breasts with sauce.

Raspberry Filling

½ teaspoon water

½ teaspoon cornstarch

5 ounces raspberries (about 1 cup)

1 tablespoon grated apple

1 tablespoon sugar

½ teaspoon lemon juice

In small bowl, blend together water and cornstarch; set aside. In small, heavy-bottomed saucepan, combine raspberries, apple, sugar and lemon juice. Crush fruit gently with a potato masher to start juices flowing. Heat to boiling over medium-high heat, then cook, stirring frequently, until mixture is no longer runny; this will take 9 to 11 minutes. Add cornstarch mixture, stirring constantly; cook for 1 to 2 minutes longer, or until thick. Cool before using.

Use this to prepare Easy Bear Claws (pg. 20), Fruit-Striped Cookie Fingers (pg. 119), or Fruit-Filled Muffins (pg. 146). Refrigerate extra filling, and use to top oatmeal or toast.

Reducing Liquid

When a recipe calls for reducing a liquid to a particular volume, it can be hard to judge without pulling it off the heat and measuring. Here's a better way. Before you start, measure water in the amount called for after reducing (so if the recipe says to boil 3 cups of liquid down to 1 cup, measure 1 cup of water). Place the measured water in the pan you'll be using, then stand a chopstick upright in the water. Use a paring knife to make a small dent or line in the chopstick at the level of the water, then discard the water and add the liquid to be reduced. When you think the liquid is getting close to the proper reduction, check it by standing the chopstick in the pan.

Camper's Delight Breakfast

This simple dish is a staple when we're camping; a pleasant hike before breakfast not only provides the main ingredient, but serves to whet the appetite.

½ to ¾ cup freshly picked raspberries (2½ to 4 ounces)

3 tablespoons vanilla yogurt or plain yogurt

2 tablespoons granola

1 teaspoon (packed) brown sugar, or maple syrup

Place freshly picked raspberries in a bowl. Top with yogurt. Sprinkle granola over yogurt, then sprinkle brown sugar or syrup over the top. Devour immediately.

Raspberry Dip

About 2 cups

This is lovely for a brunch buffet, or as a tea-time snack. Have a pretty jar of toothpicks for the pineapples and pound cake. This recipe also works well with wild strawberries.

16 ounces cream cheese, softened (reduced-fat works fine)

½ cup raspberries (about 2½ ounces)

¼ cup sour cream (reduced-fat works fine)

2 tablespoons honey

1 teaspoon vanilla extract

¼ teaspoon grated orange zest (colored rind only, with none of the white pith), optional

Dippers for serving (any or all): Pineapple chunks, pound cake cubes, vanilla wafers, pieces of chocolate bars, or assorted cookies

In food processor, combine all ingredients except dippers; process until smooth. Scrape into serving bowl. Cover and refrigerate for at least 2 hours before serving.

Raspberry Shortcakes

A classic dessert that really shows off the flavor of fresh-picked raspberries.

Shortcakes:

2 cups all-purpose flour, plus additional for rolling dough

3 tablespoons sugar

1 tablespoon baking powder

½ teaspoon salt

½ cup (1 stick) cold unsalted butter, cut into 8 pieces

⅔ cup whole milk, approximate

2 cups fresh raspberries (about 10 ounces)

½ cup sugar, or to taste

1 cup whipping cream

½ teaspoon vanilla extract

Prepare the shortcakes: Heat oven to 425°F, and line a baking sheet with kitchen parchment. In food processor, combine 2 cups flour, the sugar, baking powder and salt; pulse a few times to combine. Add cut-up butter; pulse until mixture resembles coarse meal but still has a few pea-sized pieces of butter. With motor running, add milk in a stream through the feed tube; process just until mixture comes together (don't over-process, or shortcakes will be tough).

On lightly floured worksurface, knead dough a few times to form a ball; mixture will be sticky at first, but will become less sticky as it picks up flour from the worksurface. Use a rolling pin to roll about ¾ inch thick. Cut 8 circles, using a 3-inch circular cutter (re-roll scraps once if necessary). Transfer to prepared baking sheet. Bake until dough rises and is golden brown, 10 to 15 minutes. Transfer to wire rack while you prepare the filling.

Place raspberries in mixing bowl; sprinkle with sugar, tossing gently to coat. Set aside to marinate for a few minutes. In another mixing bowl, beat whipping cream and vanilla with electric mixer until stiff peaks form.

To assemble the shortcakes, use a knife to split each shortcake horizontally. Place one half on an individual dessert plate. Top with about ¼ cup of the raspberries; place second half of shortcake on top. Dollop whipped cream over the top shortcake half; serve immediately.

Rustic Black Raspberry Tart

5 or 6 servings

This tart is a lovely presentation that is unusual enough to look like a really special treat, but it's super-easy to make. Top with some rich vanilla ice cream for a heavenly dessert.

2½ to 3 cups black raspberries (12 to 15 ounces)

½ cup sugar

3 tablespoons minute tapioca

1 tablespoon lemon juice

Ready-to-use pastry for single-crust pie

2 teaspoons butter, cut into small pieces

Heat oven to 375°F; line a rimmed baking sheet with kitchen parchment. In mixing bowl, combine raspberries, sugar, tapioca and lemon juice; stir gently. Set aside for 15 minutes. After 15 minutes, place pastry on prepared baking sheet. Pile raspberry mixture in the center, staying 1½ inches away from the edges. Working quickly, fold pastry over the edge of the filling, leaving the center exposed; the shape will be irregular, but the filling should be surrounded. Pinch overlapping areas together slightly to seal. Dot exposed filling with butter. Bake until crust is brown and filling is bubbling, 30 to 40 minutes. Let cool slightly before cutting; best served warm, the day it is made.

Ready-to-Use Pie Crust

Many recipes in this book call for "ready-to-use pastry for single- (or double-) crust pie." These days, many cooks choose to purchase ready-made pie crusts from the refrigerator case. These are already rolled out into single-crust form; simply thaw or warm them according to package directions, and use as directed. If you make your own pie crust, roll out the dough (or half the dough at once, if you've made enough for a two-crust pie) on a lightly floured worksurface, and proceed as directed.

Raspberry Jelly

4 half-pints

2¾ cups raspberry juice

Two-thirds of a 1.75-ounce box powdered pectin

½ teaspoon butter, optional (helps reduce foaming)

3⅔ cups sugar

Prepare and process as directed in Jelly Instructions (using pectin), pg. 164.

Raspberry-Balsamic Dressing

Serve this with salad made from tender greens; it's especially good if a little feta cheese is added to the salad. You could also drizzle this over cooked, sliced chicken breast that is atop a bed of spinach; garnish with sliced almonds and a few slivers of red onion.

1 cup raspberries (about 5 ounces)

5 tablespoons olive oil

2 tablespoons balsamic vinegar

1 teaspoon Dijon mustard

1 teaspoon honey

½ teaspoon salt

⅛ teaspoon white pepper

1 clove garlic, pressed or very finely minced

Purée raspberries in mini food processor or blender. Scrape into a wire-mesh strainer set over a bowl. Stir with a rubber spatula to press the purée through; discard seeds. Transfer strained purée to a half-pint jar. Add remaining ingredients. Cover tightly and shake well to blend. This will keep in the refrigerator for up to 3 weeks.

Other recipes in this book featuring raspberries or dewberries:
    Refrigerator Cookies with Dried Berries, pg. 9
    Wild Berry Vinegar, pg. 13
    Colorful Fruit Salad, pg. 30
    Fruit Terrine with Elderberry Gel, pg. 64
    Rice Pudding with Wild Berries, pg. 107
    Fruits of the Forest Pie, pg. 156
    Brambleberry Cream Sauce, pg. 157
    Six Recipes Using Wild Fruit Juice or Syrup, pgs. 158–162
    Wild Berry or Fruit Syrup, pg. 163
    Dehydrating Wild Berries and Fruits, pgs. 168–169
    As a substitute in Blackberry-Apple Crisp, pg. 15
    As a variation in Mulberry Ripple Cheesecake, pg. 104
    As a variation in Thimbleberry Smoothie, pg. 152
    As a substitute in Sautéed Fish with Thimbleberries, pg. 153

Quick ideas for using raspberries or dewberries:
    Scatter a handful on top of a mixed salad, especially one made with tender
        young greens. Serve with a blue cheese dressing or a mild vinaigrette.

ROSE HIPS *(Rosa* spp.*)*

Roses are found just about everywhere in the wild, and rose hips are easy to gather. Harvest hips when they are deeply colored and slightly soft; some foragers wait until after the first frost. Rose hips, especially the larger varieties, can be nibbled raw, but are more commonly dried to make tea, or stewed to make jam, jelly and other dishes. The fruits are loaded with vitamin C and other nutrients. The tiny seeds inside are rich in vitamin E (Steve Brill, *Identifying and Harvesting Edible and Medicinal Plants*), but they are also very bitter and may irritate the throat and stomach. If you're sampling a fresh hip, avoid eating the seeds or the dried blossom remnants.

Rose hips are so rich in vitamin C that they are used in the manufacture of some vitamin C capsules.

Most people remove the bitter seeds from rose hips before drying. To start, cut one hip in half from top to bottom; if you can easily scrape out the seeds, go ahead and process all remaining hips in this fashion, also removing the blossom remnants at the bottom. If the pulp is too sticky to remove the seeds easily, let the whole hips dry at room temperature for a few days, then try again. Don't let them get too dry, or the seeds will be even more difficult to remove. Dry split or whole hips (with the blossom remnants removed) at room temperature on a screen laid over a baking sheet, turning daily; or, dry in food dehydrator or 150°F oven (see pg. 168 for more information on dehydrating). Drying time depends on the size of the hips; split hips dry more quickly than whole hips. Store dried hips in tightly sealed glass jars in a dark location.

To make rose hip purée or juice, remove the stems and blossom ends, then measure the hips and place in a non-aluminum pot. For purée, add 1 cup water per quart of hips; for juice, add 3 cups water per quart of hips. (For a nice variation, use apple juice instead of water.) Heat to boiling, then reduce the heat; cover and simmer until soft, about 15 minutes, gently crushing the hips with a potato masher near the end of cooking.

For purée, process the cooked hips through a cone-shaped colander, or rub through a fine wire-mesh strainer; discard the seeds and skin. (I don't use a food mill with rose hips, because too many of the bitter seeds get into the purée.) **For juice,** transfer the mixture to a strainer lined with doubled, dampened cheesecloth and let it drip for 30 minutes; don't squeeze the fruit because some bitter seeds may get through the cheesecloth. Processed this way, a quart of rose hips will yield about 2 cups of lovely, pinkish-red purée, or about 2½ cups pinkish-red juice.

Rose Hip Tea
Per serving

Combine 1 tablespoon dried rose hips, or 2 tablespoons fresh rose hips, in a saucepan with 1 cup of cold water. Heat to boiling, then remove from heat, cover and let steep for 10 to 15 minutes. Strain and sweeten to taste with sugar, honey or maple syrup; serve with a lemon wedge if you like.

Marlin with Rose Hip Glaze

This sweet-tangy glaze would also be good with pork loin chops or tenderloin.

½ cup rose hip purée

3 tablespoons (packed) brown sugar

2 tablespoons Asian fish sauce

1 teaspoon butter

½ teaspoon finely minced fresh gingerroot

1 tablespoon freshly squeezed lime juice

4 pieces marlin, ¾ inch thick (6 to 8 ounces each)

1 tablespoon olive oil

In small non-aluminum saucepan, stir together purée, brown sugar, fish sauce, butter and gingerroot. Cook over medium heat, stirring frequently, until thickened, about 10 minutes. Transfer half of the sauce to a small bowl; stir in lime juice and set aside.

Heat oven to 400°F. Rinse fish; pat dry with paper towels. In heavy, oven-safe skillet, heat olive oil over medium-high heat until shimmering. Add fish in a single layer; cook for 2 minutes, then turn with spatula. Spread the mixture remaining in the saucepan evenly over each fish piece. Transfer skillet to oven; cook until the center is just opaque, 6 to 8 minutes. Transfer to serving plate. Serve with remaining sauce mixture.

 Fish sauce is found in the Asian section of large supermarkets, or at specialty markets. I prefer Three Crabs brand from Vietnam; some excellent sauces also come from Thailand. The fish sauce adds a lot of flavor depth, but if you don't have any, substitute Japanese soy sauce such as Kikkoman.

Rose Hip Jelly (pectin added)

2½ cups rose hip juice

¼ cup lemon juice

Half of a 1.75-ounce box powdered pectin

½ teaspoon butter, optional (helps reduce foaming)

2½ cups sugar

Prepare and process as directed in Jelly Instructions (using pectin), pg. 164.

Rose Hip-Apple Jelly (no added pectin)

3 half-pints

Tart apples add both flavor and pectin to this jelly.

½ pound fresh rose hips, blossom ends removed before weighing

½ pound Granny Smith apples, cored and chopped

1 lemon

2 cups sugar, approximate

Please read "Jelly Instructions for Fruits with Natural Pectin" on pg. 166 to learn about testing for doneness. In non-aluminum saucepan, combine rose hips and chopped apples. Add water to cover completely. Cut the lemon into quarters, and remove the rind (including the white pith) and seeds. Add lemon flesh to pan with rose hips. Heat to boiling over high heat. Reduce heat so mixture is simmering, then cover and simmer until all fruit is very soft, about 30 minutes. Mash with a potato masher.

Line a wire-mesh strainer with two thicknesses of damp cheesecloth; place over a non-aluminum pot. Spoon fruit mixture into cheesecloth; let drip for 2 hours without squeezing or stirring. At the end of the 2 hours, prepare 3 half-pint canning jars, bands and new lids as directed on pg. 171.

Discard pulp in cheesecloth. Measure the juice; you should have about 2½ cups. Place measured juice in a non-aluminum pot that holds 3 or 4 quarts. For each cup of juice, measure ⅞ cup of sugar. Heat juice to boiling over medium-high heat. Add sugar and cook, stirring constantly, until sugar dissolves. Increase heat to high and cook, skimming off any foam and stirring frequently, until jelly passes one or more of the doneness tests on pg. 166; this typically takes 10 to 15 minutes.

Once the jelly is done, skim any foam off the surface and pour it, while still hot, into the prepared canning jars; seal with prepared lids and bands. Process in a water-bath canner (pg. 171) for 10 minutes, or store in the refrigerator.

 Slightly underripe crabapples can be substituted for the Granny Smith apples; remove the stems and blossom ends but don't bother removing the seeds.

Rose Hip Soup

This dish is common in the Scandinavian countries, where it is often served to soothe sore throats and colds. It can be served hot or cold; when served cold, it is sometimes diluted with water or apple juice and served as a beverage.

3 cups rose hip juice

2 tablespoons honey, or to taste

2 tablespoons freshly squeezed lemon juice, or to taste

¼ cup ground almonds

1 tablespoon potato starch, or 2 teaspoons cornstarch

1 tablespoon cold water

¼ cup sour cream

Fresh mint sprigs as a garnish

In a non-aluminum saucepan, combine rose hip juice, honey and lemon juice. Heat to boiling, then reduce heat and add ground almonds; simmer for about 5 minutes. In small bowl, blend potato starch and water, then whisk into simmering soup. Cook, whisking constantly, until mixture bubbles and thickens. Taste for seasoning, and adjust with more honey or lemon juice if you like. Divide mixture into 4 bowls. Add a tablespoon of sour cream to each serving; garnish with mint sprig.

Other recipes in this book featuring rose hips:
Six Recipes Using Wild Fruit Juice or Syrup, pgs. 158–162
Wild Berry or Fruit Syrup, pg. 163

Quick ideas for using rose hips:
Stir a few tablespoons of the purée into applesauce.
Mix 1 part rose hip juice with 2 parts apple juice; sweeten to taste, and serve as a breakfast drink.
Add a few tablespoons purée to the mixture when making a smoothie.
Use a mix of one part rose hip juice to three parts water when brewing black or green tea.

RUSSIAN OLIVES *(Elaeagnus angustifolia)*

Fruits from the Russian olive tree are not used very often; it's more of a curiosity than a foraging staple. One advantage is that the trees produce abundant fruit, so it's quite easy to harvest enough to experiment with. Fruits can be eaten raw or cooked, although the dry, mealy nature makes them fairly unpalatable when raw.

When harvesting Russian olives, choose those that are yellow or cream-colored; underripe green fruits are very astringent. The fruits have a fairly large pit, which is very hard and inedible; it can be removed by cooking the fruits, then straining and puréeing the flesh.

Russian olive flesh is dry and mealy, but it has a sweet flavor and aroma that is reminiscent of apples.

To make Russian olive purée, place fruits in a saucepan, with enough water to not quite cover. Heat to boiling; reduce heat, cover, and simmer for 10 minutes to soften the fruit. Cool slightly, then process the fruits through a food mill. The pits, which are long and narrow with pointed ends, are thick enough to prevent all of the pulp from going through the mill. Once you've gotten as much flesh through the food mill as possible, scrape out the seedy pulp remaining in the mill and place it in a mixing bowl. Add just enough water to loosen the mixture. Now place this into a colander or some other device that has holes small enough to prevent the seeds from going through; I use the top half of a vegetable steamer saucepan. Stir the mixture with a rubber spatula (or use your hands), pressing the soft flesh through the holes; add a little more water if necessary, and keep at it until you've gotten as much flesh separated as possible. Processed in this fashion, 2 cups of whole fruits (about 8 ounces) will yield about 1 cup of purée. The purée has a fairly solid, almost dry texture, and is pale greenish-gray.

Coarse Russian Olive Mustard

About 1¼ cups

Homemade mustard is easy to make, and Russian olive purée makes an interesting base. It provides a good texture, and a hint of sweetness.

½ cup Russian olive purée

⅓ cup white wine vinegar

¼ cup yellow mustard seeds

3 tablespoons brown mustard seeds

1 tablespoon dry sherry

2 teaspoons honey

1 teaspoon salt

¼ teaspoon ground turmeric

¼ teaspoon white pepper, optional (adds heat)

Pinch of ground nutmeg

Combine all ingredients in a glass or ceramic mixing bowl; stir well. Cover and refrigerate overnight.

The next day, transfer the mustard to a blender; add a little water if it is too firm. Process until the mustard is well-blended but still somewhat coarse; add additional water if needed. Taste and adjust seasonings as you like; you may want it sweeter, hotter or more salty. Store in a tightly covered jar in the refrigerator; it will keep for about a month. If it becomes stiff after a while, stir in a little water.

Oatmeal Muffins with Russian Olive

6 muffins

This recipe brings out the natural apple-like sweetness of the Russian olive purée.

½ cup Russian olive purée

1 egg

¼ cup orange juice

¼ cup sugar

2 tablespoons vegetable oil

½ cup quick-cooking rolled oats (not instant)

½ cup all-purpose flour

1½ teaspoons baking powder

½ teaspoon cinnamon

¼ teaspoon baking soda

½ cup dried cranberries (home-dried wild cranberries, or purchased craisins)

Heat oven to 375°F. Spray 6-cup muffin pan with nonstick spray, or line with muffin papers; set aside. In mixing bowl, combine Russian olive purée and egg; beat together with a fork. Add orange juice, sugar and vegetable oil; beat until well-combined. Stir in oatmeal. Place a wire-mesh strainer over the bowl; add flour, baking powder, cinnamon and baking soda. Shake strainer to sift into the bowl; stir with a wooden spoon just until moistened. Add dried cranberries and stir gently. Divide mixture evenly into prepared muffin cups. Bake until a toothpick inserted into the center of a muffin comes out clean, about 25 minutes. Remove muffin tin from oven and let cool for 15 minutes before removing muffins.

Quick ideas for using Russian olive purée:
> Add some of the purée to a smoothie or malt.
> Cook purée with diced peaches or other fruit, and add sugar to taste, to make an interesting fruit sauce.
> Try using some of the purée to replace applesauce in recipes; it's much more dry than applesauce, so don't replace all of the applesauce (or, adjust the recipe to increase the liquid).

SERVICEBERRIES *(Amelanchier* spp.)

Found in one form or another throughout our area, serviceberries are surprisingly unfamiliar to many people. But the fruits are not showy, so they're easy to miss unless you're looking for them.

Technically a pome, serviceberries have a small crown on the bottom (like an apple), and several small, soft seeds. The seeds can be eaten with no trouble, and I never bother taking them out, but some cooks prefer to strain cooked serviceberries to remove the seeds. I typically use the fruits whole, in much the same way that I use blueberries or huckleberries. They're also a fantastic trail nibble; the sight of a laden serviceberry tree brings a smile to me when I'm hiking in the summer. They're sweet, with a subtle almond-like flavor, and they provide much-needed refreshment and energy on a hot July day.

Serviceberries were a staple in the diets of American Indians in our area, and were mentioned by explorers Meriwether Lewis and William Clark in the diaries of their western travels.

Even though many of the fruits are up out of reach, it's pretty easy to collect a good quantity of serviceberries if you find an area with several trees. Birds and other wildlife depend on serviceberries for food, so don't try too hard to get at the fruits you can't reach; leave them for the waxwings, robins, grosbeaks and magpies. (I have fond memories of picking serviceberries from a small tree that was heavy with them, and dodging the cedar waxwings that were gorging themselves on fruit just a few feet from me.)

Serviceberries can be used whole for baking, or turned into jam; they can also be dehydrated, for use in baked goods or trail mix. They are easy to freeze; wash the fruits and pat them dry, then spread on a baking sheet in a single layer. Freeze overnight, then transfer to plastic containers and seal tightly.

Serviceberry or Blueberry Freezer Jam   4 half-pints

This jam is easy to make because the fruit is not cooked; commercial pectin is cooked separately, then stirred into the fruit mixture.

1 quart serviceberries or blueberries

2¾ cups sugar

**Two-thirds of a 1.75-ounce box powdered pectin
   (see pg. 164 for information on dividing pectin)**

½ cup water

2 tablespoons lemon juice

Prepare 4 half-pint canning jars, bands and lids as described on pg. 171, or have clean plastic freezer containers ready (see tip below). Chop fruit to medium consistency in food processor (don't overprocess; jam should have small fruit chunks in it). Measure 1¾ cups chopped fruit; use any leftover fruit to top ice cream or cook in other recipes. Place measured fruit and the sugar in a large ceramic or Pyrex mixing bowl. Stir well; set aside for 10 minutes, stirring several times with a wooden spoon.

After fruit has rested for 10 minutes, prepare pectin. In small non-aluminum saucepan, combine pectin, water and lemon juice; stir well (mixture may be lumpy). Heat to a full, rolling boil over high heat, stirring constantly. Cook at a rolling boil for 1 minute, stirring constantly. Pour pectin mixture into fruit in bowl. Stir constantly with a wooden spoon until sugar is completely dissolved and no longer grainy, about 3 minutes; a few grains may remain, but the mixture should no longer look cloudy (or the jam will be cloudy).

Pour into prepared jars or containers, leaving ½ inch headspace; cover with clean lids. Let stand at room temperature for 24 hours; the jam should set (it may be softer than regular jam, especially at first; that's okay). If jam is not set, refrigerate for several days until set before using or freezing. Use within 3 weeks, or freeze until needed; thaw frozen jam in refrigerator.

 Special plastic containers, designed especially for freezing, are available with the canning supplies at the supermarket.

Serviceberry and Ricotta Brunch Ring   12 to 16 servings

This delicious cake gets extra moistness from ricotta cheese. The almonds add a nice texture, and point up the subtly nutty taste of the serviceberries.

½ cup (1 stick) unsalted butter, softened

1 cup sugar

1 container (15 ounces) ricotta cheese (reduced-fat works fine)

½ cup whole or 2% milk

2 eggs

1 teaspoon vanilla extract

2½ cups flour

1 tablespoon baking powder

½ teaspoon salt

1½ cups fresh serviceberries (about 6½ ounces)

1 cup finely chopped slivered almonds (about 4½ ounces)

Powdered sugar for dusting, optional

Heat oven to 350°F. Grease and flour a 12-cup bundt pan or an angel-food cake pan; set aside.

In large mixing bowl, cream butter with electric mixer for about 1 minute. Add sugar; beat for another minute. Add ricotta cheese, milk, eggs and vanilla; beat on medium speed for 2 minutes, scraping bowl several times. Combine flour, baking powder and salt in sifter or wire-mesh strainer; sift or shake mixture into mixing bowl. Add serviceberries and almonds, and stir together with wooden spoon until well-mixed.

Spoon mixture into prepared pan, evening out and smoothing the top. Bake in center of oven until a toothpick inserted into the center comes out clean, about an hour. Cool on a wire rack for 20 minutes, then remove from pan; put the prettiest side up. Dust top with powdered sugar, if you like. Cool until just warm before slicing, or cool completely and serve at room temperature.

If you have leftovers, wrap tightly in plastic wrap, then wrap again in foil, smoothing tightly. Seal the seams with freezer tape, and freeze up to 3 months.

Serviceberry and Wild Rice Muffins

6 muffins

Wild rice is a natural with serviceberries in these hearty muffins.

³/₄ cup all-purpose flour

¹/₄ cup sugar

1 teaspoon baking powder

¹/₄ teaspoon salt

¹/₂ cup fresh or previously frozen serviceberries (about 2 ounces)

¹/₄ cup whole or 2% milk

2 tablespoons butter, melted and cooled slightly

1 egg

¹/₃ cup cooked wild rice

Heat oven to 350°F. Line 6-cup muffin pan with paper liners, or spray with nonstick spray; set aside. Place wire-mesh strainer over large mixing bowl. Add flour, sugar, baking powder and salt; shake into bowl to sift together. Place serviceberries in small bowl; spoon about 2 teaspoons of the flour mixture over them, stirring to coat.

In measuring cup, beat together milk, butter and egg. Pour milk mixture into flour mixture and fold together with rubber spatula. Add floured serviceberries and wild rice; fold together. Spoon into prepared muffin cups. Bake until lightly browned and a toothpick inserted into the center of a muffin comes out clean, 25 to 30 minutes.

Serviceberry Filling

About ½ cup; easily increased

1 teaspoon water

¹/₂ teaspoon cornstarch

5¹/₂ ounces fresh or previously serviceberries (about 1¹/₄ cups)

¹/₄ cup sugar

1 tablespoon grated apple

In small bowl, blend together water and cornstarch; set aside. In small, heavy-bottomed saucepan, combine serviceberries, sugar and apple. Crush fruit gently with a potato masher to start juices flowing. Heat to boiling over medium-high heat, then cook, stirring frequently and mashing once more, until mixture is no longer runny; this will take 7 to 9 minutes. Add cornstarch mixture, stirring constantly; cook for about 1½ minutes longer, or until thick. Cool before using.

Use this to prepare Easy Bear Claws (pg. 20), Fruit-Striped Cookie Fingers (pg. 119), or Fruit-Filled Muffins (pg. 146). Refrigerate extra filling, and use to top oatmeal or toast.

Serviceberry Pie
1 pie (6 to 8 servings)

Chopped almonds add a wonderful texture to this luscious pie.

3 cups fresh or previously frozen serviceberries, divided (12 to 13 ounces)

⅔ cup sugar

3 tablespoons cornstarch

1 tablespoon lemon juice

1 tablespoon butter, cut into several pieces

½ teaspoon cinnamon

A pinch of salt

A few drops almond extract, optional

Ready-to-use pastry for double-crust pie

⅓ cup finely chopped almonds

1 egg yolk, beaten with 1 tablespoon cold water

In medium non-aluminum saucepan, combine 1 cup of serviceberries with the sugar, cornstarch and lemon juice; stir to mix. Heat to boiling over medium heat, stirring constantly; cook, stirring constantly, until liquid clears and thickens. Remove from heat; stir in butter, cinnamon, salt and extract. Let cool for about 5 minutes, then add remaining 2 cups serviceberries and set aside until completely cool, about 1 hour.

When the serviceberry mixture has cooled, heat oven to 400°F. Fit one pastry into ungreased pie plate. Scatter almonds evenly in crust. Scrape cooled serviceberry mixture into pie plate. Moisten edges of pastry in pie plate with a little cold water, then top with second pastry. Seal, trim and flute edges. Cut 6 to 8 inch-long slits in the crust. Place pie on baking sheet (to catch drips). Brush top with beaten egg. Bake until crust is golden and filling bubbles through slits, about 30 minutes. Transfer to rack to cool; best served warm.

Serviceberry Pudding Cake

This is equally appropriate for breakfast or dessert. It's fabulous when still warm from the oven, but it's also good served at room temperature.

½ cup white sugar

3 tablespoons cold water

2 tablespoons lemon juice

1½ teaspoons cornstarch

2 cups fresh or frozen serviceberries (about 8 ounces)

1 cup all-purpose flour

½ cup (packed) golden brown sugar

2 teaspoons baking powder

1 teaspoon salt

1 egg

½ cup whole milk or buttermilk

6 tablespoons unsalted butter, melted and cooled slightly

1 teaspoon vanilla extract

Heat oven to 375°F. Spray an 8-inch-square baking dish with nonstick spray; set aside. In medium non-aluminum saucepan, stir together white sugar, water, lemon juice and cornstarch. Heat over medium heat, stirring constantly, until sugar dissolves, about 3 minutes. Add serviceberries; simmer for about a minute, stirring occasionally. Remove from heat.

In medium bowl, stir together flour, brown sugar, baking powder and salt. In large mixing bowl, combine egg, milk, butter and vanilla; beat with whisk until smooth. Add flour mixture; whisk until smooth. Scrape mixture into prepared baking dish, spreading evenly. Pour serviceberry mixture evenly over the top. Bake until a table knife inserted into the center comes out clean, about 30 minutes. Set pan on rack to cool for 5 or 10 minutes before serving. Cake can be cooled, then covered tightly with foil and kept at room temperature for up to 2 days.

Substitutions: Blueberries or huckleberries can be substituted for the serviceberries.

If using frozen serviceberries, measure them while still frozen, then rinse briefly under running water and spread out on a baking sheet lined with paper towels.

Microwave Oatmeal with Serviceberries and Nuts

Easy, quick and filling, this is the perfect breakfast.

⅔ cup water

⅓ cup old-fashioned rolled oats

2 to 3 tablespoons fresh serviceberries

2 drops of vanilla extract

1 tablespoon chopped pecans

Honey, maple syrup or brown sugar to taste

Cream or whole milk to taste, optional

In microwave-safe bowl that holds 2 to 3 cups, combine water, oats, serviceberries and vanilla. Microwave on high, uncovered, until oatmeal is thick and most of the water has been absorbed, 1½ to 2½ minutes. Remove bowl from microwave; stir well and let stand until all water is absorbed, 30 seconds to 1 minute. Sprinkle with pecans; top with honey and cream to taste.

 Prepare this one bowl at a time; cooking times will change if you put two or more in the microwave at the same time. Use old-fashioned rolled oatmeal, rather than quick-cooking oatmeal, for the best texture.

Other recipes in this book featuring serviceberries:
Refrigerator Cookies with Dried Berries, pg. 9
Cookies with Dried Fruit, Nuts and White Chocolate Chips, pg. 28
Fruits of the Forest Pie, pg. 156
Dehydrating Wild Berries and Fruits, pgs. 168–169
As a substitute in Blackberry-Apple Crisp, pg. 15
As a substitute in Blueberry Streusel Muffins, pg. 21
As a substitute in Individual Currant Cheesecakes, pg. 57
As a variation in Thimbleberry Smoothie, pg. 152

Quick ideas for using serviceberries:
Substitute serviceberries for fresh blueberries in recipes. Serviceberries are not quite as juicy as blueberries, so you may need to increase the liquid slightly.
Use 1¼ cups of serviceberries in place of one of the sliced apples when making apple pie.

SPICEBUSH, NORTHERN (Lindera benzoin)

If you encounter a spicebush shrub in the woods, you'll know it; the entire plant has a pleasantly spicy smell that is similar to allspice. The berries—technically drupes—can be used as a substitute for allspice, either whole or ground. They work well in chutney, marinades, jam and sauces. Even the leaves can be dried, then used to flavor stews and marinades; they have a more subtle flavor than the fruits.

The fruits tend to develop a musty flavor if stored at room temperature for more than a few weeks; for best results, keep them in the refrigerator or freezer until needed. For ground spicebush, use a coffee grinder or mortar and pestle to grind them just before use; the ground spice loses its flavor quickly.

Jerk Marinade
Enough marinade for 2 to 3 pounds meat

"Jerk" cooking is a Caribbean specialty that uses a spicy, highly seasoned marinade to flavor cuts like flank steak. Here's a jerk-style marinade that uses spicebush berries; the heat has been toned down a bit, so if you like really spicy jerk, substitute habañero peppers for the jalapeño.

¼ cup freshly squeezed lime juice

¼ cup vegetable oil

2 tablespoons soy sauce

2 tablespoons molasses

2 teaspoons fresh thyme leaves, or 1 teaspoon dried

1 teaspoon coarse black pepper

12 whole spicebush berries

3 cloves garlic

2 green onions, cut into 1-inch pieces (discard roots)

1 or 2 jalapeño peppers, stems and seeds removed

1-inch cube of peeled fresh gingerroot

Combine all ingredients in blender; process until smooth.

To use, combine marinade and meat in heavy zipper-style plastic bag; seal and turn to coat meat with marinade. Marinate in refrigerator, turning occasionally. Flank steak or pork roast should be marinated at least 4 hours, and as long as overnight; pork chops or chicken pieces should be marinated 2 to 4 hours. After marinating, remove meat from marinade and broil or grill over direct, high heat.

Spicy Plum Chutney

This is delicious alongside grilled or broiled meats and fish, and with curry dishes.

4 whole cardamom pods

6 whole spicebush berries

3 cups cut-up plum pieces (½-inch pieces), wild or domestic

1 cup diced red bell pepper (¼-inch dice)

¾ cup diced onion (¼-inch dice)

¼ cup golden raisins or purchased dried currants

¼ cup (packed) brown sugar

¼ cup balsamic vinegar or red-wine vinegar

1 tablespoon minced crystallized ginger (found in the spice aisle)

½ teaspoon yellow mustard seeds

½ teaspoon salt

¼ teaspoon hot red pepper flakes

Split cardamom pods and transfer seeds to mortar; add spicebush and crush until mixture is coarse. Combine spice mixture with remaining ingredients in heavy-bottomed non-aluminum saucepan. Heat to boiling over high heat. Reduce heat so mixture simmers steadily and cook until thickened and syrupy, about 45 minutes. Stir frequently, especially near the end of the cooking time, to prevent sticking. Cool and transfer to a clean pint jar; store in refrigerator for up to 3 weeks.

Substitutions: If you have wild plums but no spicebush berries, substitute 2 whole allspice berries, or ¼ teaspoon ground allspice, for the spicebush berries. You could also substitute wild cherries for the plums (if you have the patience to pit 3 cups!).

Other recipes in this book featuring spicebush:
Tart Mountain Ash Jelly, pg. 101

Quick ideas for using spicebush:
Substitute whole spicebush berries for whole allspice in recipes; use twice as many spicebush berries as the quantity listed for allspice.
Add a few whole spicebush berries to marinades for beef, pork or venison.
When making applesauce, add 3 or 4 whole spicebush berries to the apples during cooking. If you're straining or puréeing the applesauce after cooking, leave the berries in the mixture; otherwise, fish them out with a spoon afterwards.

STRAWBERRIES *(Fragaria virginiana, F. vesca)*

It's fun to watch the reaction of someone who's tasting a wild strawberry for the first time. Wonderment over the tiny size of the fruit changes to awed delight when they taste it. "I never knew strawberries could taste like this!" is a common response—quickly followed by a dive to the ground in search of more strawberries.

Wild strawberries are so tiny that it is hard to gather enough to make, say, a batch of jam—and they're so delicious that it's tough to stop eating them on the spot, rather than putting them in the berry pail. I've never made wild strawberry jelly, because I've never wanted to sacrifice enough wild strawberries to make the juice. However, if you've hit the strawberry jackpot and want to make jelly (or other recipes prepared with juice), follow the instructions for making mulberry juice on pg. 102.

The hardest part about picking wild strawberries to make a pie or jam is refraining from devouring them all on the spot, before they even hit the berry bucket—they're that good!

When you're using wild strawberries in recipes that were developed for domestic strawberries, don't rely on per-cup measurements. Wild strawberries are so much smaller than their domesticated cousins that they pack more tightly into the cup, so you'd be using more strawberries (by weight) than the recipe probably intended. Domestic strawberries are also less juicy, so liquid will probably need to be reduced when substituting wild strawberries because they have so much more juice.

Wild strawberries can easily be frozen, but the texture will be soft when they are thawed. Spread them in a single layer on a baking sheet or plate that has been lined with waxed paper; cover with plastic wrap. Freeze overnight, then pack into tightly sealed plastic containers and store in the coldest part of the freezer; use within a few months for best flavor.

Strawberry Freezer Jam   4 half-pints

Freezer jam is not cooked, so it has a fresher taste and a vibrant color. It is a little softer than cooked jam. Wild strawberries make the best freezer jam in the world, but if you can't bear to part with enough to make a full batch of this, see pg. 143 for small-batch instructions.

> **1¼ pounds fresh wild strawberries (about 3½ cups)**
>
> **4 cups sugar**
>
> **1 pouch Certo liquid pectin**
>
> **2 tablespoons freshly squeezed lemon juice**

Wash and hull strawberries. Pulse on-and-off in a food processor until fruit is finely chopped (not puréed); if you prefer, mash with a potato masher. Measure finely chopped strawberries; transfer exactly 2 cups to a large ceramic or Pyrex mixing bowl. If you have any leftover chopped strawberries, enjoy them over ice cream; don't use more than 2 cups for this recipe.

Add sugar and stir well; set aside for 10 minutes, stirring several times with a wooden spoon. Meanwhile, stir pectin and lemon juice together in a small bowl. After strawberries and sugar have stood for 10 minutes, add pectin mixture to strawberries, scraping to get all the pectin into the berries. Stir continuously for 3 minutes; sugar should be completely dissolved. Cover bowl tightly with plastic wrap. Let stand at room temperature for 24 hours; jam should be softly set.

When jam has set for 24 hours, prepare 4 half-pint canning jars, bands and lids as described on pg. 171, or have clean plastic freezer containers ready (see tip below). Divide fruit between prepared containers, leaving ½ inch headspace. Cover and refrigerate. Use within 3 weeks, or freeze until needed; thaw frozen jam in refrigerator.

 Special plastic containers, designed especially for freezing, are available with the canning supplies at the supermarket.

Small-Batch Freezer Jam

If you don't have enough berries to make a full batch, you can make a half-batch. The only tricky part is measuring half of the pectin. It is extremely thick and clings to the measuring spoon or cup, making accurate measuring difficult. To make it easier, mix up the full batch of pectin and lemon juice in a measuring cup, then use exactly half of that in the strawberry mixture. The lemon juice makes it easier to measure.

Place 1 cup of finely chopped strawberries into a large mixing bowl. Add 2 cups sugar; stir and let stand as directed above. Mix the full pouch of pectin with 2 tablespoons lemon juice in a glass measuring cup (when I tested it, it came out to ½ cup, but the pectin formula may change in the future so you need to check this each time). After strawberries and sugar have stood for 10 minutes, pour *exactly half* of the pectin mixture into the strawberry mixture (I poured pectin into the strawberry mixture until there was ¼ cup left in the measuring cup). Proceed as directed. Discard remaining pectin if you don't have another use for it.

Mixed Greens with Strawberries, Honey Pecans and Blue Cheese

4 first-course servings; easily increased

Here's a salad with a fabulous combination of flavors and textures. It serves four as a first course for a special dinner, or two if presented as the center item for a luncheon. Preparation is divided into three parts; you can prepare the nuts and dressing a day or two in advance.

Honey pecans:

¾ cup pecan halves

1 tablespoon honey

2 teaspoons butter, melted

A pinch of curry powder

Vinaigrette:

⅓ cup extra-virgin olive oil

2 tablespoons white wine vinegar

1 teaspoon orange juice

¾ teaspoon Dijon mustard

½ teaspoon salt

⅛ teaspoon finely minced or grated fresh gingerroot

A few grindings of black pepper

Salad:

3 slices thick-cut bacon

6 cups tender mixed salad greens

3 thin slices red onion, quartered after slicing

½ cup blue cheese crumbles

⅔ to ¾ cup fresh wild strawberries (4 to 5 ounces)

Prepare the nuts: Heat oven to 425°F. Line a small baking sheet with foil; spray with nonstick spray. In a small bowl, stir together the pecans, honey, butter and curry powder. Spread out on foil-lined baking sheet. Bake until nuts are lightly browned, 5 to 7 minutes, stirring twice. Remove from oven before they are as brown as you would like because they will continue to cook for a few minutes after you remove them from the oven. Let nuts cool completely; can be prepared a day or two in advance (store cooled nuts in air-tight container at room temperature).

Make the vinaigrette: In a small jar, combine oil, vinegar, orange juice, mustard, salt, gingerroot and pepper; cover and shake well to blend. Taste for flavor balance and adjust if necessary, adding more oil or vinegar, or more salt and pepper, to suit your taste. Set aside until needed. This can sit at room temperature for a few hours, or be refrigerated for several days; if refrigerated, bring to room temperature an hour before serving.

Finish preparation and assemble the salad: Shortly before serving, cut the bacon cross-wise (across the width) into ⅜-inch pieces. In medium skillet, fry over medium heat until crisp, stirring frequently. Transfer with slotted spoon to a plate lined with paper towels; blot surface with another paper towel.

Divide greens evenly between 4 salad-sized serving plates, or 2 dinner-sized plates. Sprinkle evenly with onions, breaking up the rings a bit. Top with bacon; sprinkle cheese over the bacon. Carefully place the strawberries on top, arranging attractively. Scatter honey pecans over all. Shake the dressing again, then drizzle over salads. Serve immediately.

Strawberry Filling
About ½ cup; easily increased

This is a nice use for a small harvest of wild strawberries.

½ teaspoon water

½ teaspoon cornstarch

6 ounces fresh or previously frozen wild strawberries (about 1 cup)

2 teaspoons sugar

1 teaspoon lemon juice

In small bowl, blend together water and cornstarch; set aside. In small, heavy-bottomed non-aluminum saucepan, combine strawberries, sugar and lemon juice. Crush fruit gently with a potato masher to start juices flowing. Heat to boiling over medium-high heat, then cook, stirring frequently, until mixture is no longer runny; this will take 8 to 10 minutes. Add cornstarch mixture, stirring constantly; cook for about 1 minute longer, or until thick. Cool before using.

Use this to prepare Easy Bear Claws (pg. 20), Fruit-Striped Cookie Fingers (pg. 119), or Fruit-Filled Muffins (pg. 146). Refrigerate extra filling, and use to top oatmeal or toast.

Fruit-Filled Muffins

These make a nice, quick breakfast. Freeze any muffins you won't be eating within a few days, wrapping them tightly in plastic wrap and then in foil.

1³/₄ cups all-purpose flour

¹/₂ to ²/₃ cup sugar, depending on how sweet you want the muffins

2 teaspoons baking powder

¹/₄ teaspoon salt

²/₃ cup whole or 2% milk

¹/₃ cup vegetable oil

1 egg

1 teaspoon vanilla extract

¹/₂ cup Strawberry Filling (pg. 145), or other wild fruit filling (see "Filling options" below)

Heat oven to 375°F. Line a 12-cup muffin tin with paper liners, or spray with nonstick spray; set aside. Place wire-mesh strainer over large mixing bowl. Add flour, sugar, baking powder and salt; shake strainer to sift mixture into bowl. In measuring cup or small bowl, beat together milk, oil, egg and vanilla. Add milk mixture to flour mixture; stir with a wooden spoon until just moistened. Spoon half of the batter evenly into prepared muffin cups. Drop about 1 teaspoon of the filling onto the center of the muffin batter, keeping away from the edges; spoon remaining batter over filling. Bake until golden brown and springy to the touch, 20 to 25 minutes.

Filling options: This recipe works with any of the following fillings: Blackberry (pg. 14), Blueberry (pg. 23), Crabapple (pg. 45), Green Gooseberry (pg. 71), Ground Cherry (pg. 82), Mulberry (pg. 105), Nannyberry (pg. 111), Plum (pg. 117), Raspberry (pg. 121), Serviceberry (pg. 136), Strawberry (pg. 145), or Thimbleberry (pg. 154).

Strawberries and Shortbread

4 servings

This simple, but interesting, dessert was inspired by a recipe from the well-known French chef, Jacques Pépin.

2 cups fresh wild strawberries (about 12 ounces), divided

2 teaspoons sugar, or to taste

¼ teaspoon vanilla extract

4 ounces shortbread cookies

⅓ cup crème fraîche or sour cream

2 tablespoons (packed) brown sugar

4 sprigs fresh mint for garnish, optional

In mini food processor, process half of the strawberries with the sugar and vanilla; transfer to small bowl. Slice remaining strawberries, then gently stir into the strawberry purée. Place shortbread cookies in plastic bag, and crush coarsely with rolling pin. (If preparing in advance, cover and refrigerate strawberries until serving time; set crushed cookies aside.)

To serve, spoon about 2 tablespoons of the strawberry mixture into each of 4 wine glasses or parfait dishes. Divide shortbread crumbs evenly among glasses. Top evenly with remaining strawberry mixture. Spoon crème fraîche evenly on top; sprinkle with brown sugar and garnish with mint sprig. Let stand 5 to 10 minutes before serving.

Other recipes in this book featuring wild strawberries:
Refrigerator Cookies with Dried Berries, pg. 9
Wild Berry Vinegar, pg. 13
Strawberry-Gooseberry Dessert Sauce, pg. 75
Dehydrating Wild Berries and Fruits, pgs. 168–169
As a substitute in Wild Blueberry Pancakes, pg. 24
As a substitute in Raspberry Dip, pg. 122
As a variation in Thimbleberry Smoothie, pg. 152

Quick ideas for using wild strawberries:
Sprinkle over cold cereal before adding milk and sugar; way better
than sliced bananas!
Add to mixed fruit salads.
Add a few to an apple pie, for a delightful difference.
Enjoy them over ice cream, or in a bowl with a little cream or yogurt.

SUMAC: SMOOTH, STAGHORN and FRAGRANT
(Rhus glabra, R. typhina and R. aromatica)

Smooth and staghorn sumac trees are the most familiar members of the sumac family, but fragrant sumac, which grows as a shrub rather than a tree, is also found in our area; it has fuzzy, reddish-orange fruits that can be used in the same way as the larger, pyramid-shaped clusters found on smooth and staghorn sumac.

Fragrant sumac berries are ripe in midsummer, usually before smooth and staghorn sumac clusters. All should be harvested when they're fully ripe and a bit sticky; if you wait too long, rain will wash away the flavor and the berries will dry up. Use a pruning snippers to cut off entire clusters; it doesn't hurt the plant, because they reproduce by underground runners.

Sumac is probably the first unfamiliar wild edible that kids learn about. "Sumac-ade" is a staple at summer camps across our area; it's easy for kids to identify and pick the bright reddish-orange clusters, and fun to make a tasty beverage out of them.

When working with staghorn and smooth sumac, you can use the whole cluster, or pick the berries off the stems; picking is more work, but it eliminates any dirt, spiders or other undesirables that may be hiding inside the cluster. For storage, freeze picked berries in heavyweight plastic bags; the frozen berries retain all their flavor and can be used later to make sumac juice, tea or whatever you like. Clusters can be frozen as well, but they take up a lot more room; as an option, you can place them in a loosely sealed paper bag and let them dry, then use them in winter to make tea (they won't make very good juice after they've been dried). Sumac berries have tiny hairs that are somewhat irritating to the throat; they can be removed by straining the liquid through a paper coffee filter.

To make sumac juice, use fresh berry clusters that are still sticky; frozen berries or clusters work as well, as long as they were sticky before freezing. Place clusters or picked berries in a soup pot or plastic bucket, then add cold water just to cover. Squeeze the berries with your hands, and rub them up and down along the sides of the pot as though scrubbing on a washboard. Do this for a few minutes, then let the mixture stand for a few minutes and repeat. I usually let them soak for 10 to 20 minutes after that; I want to extract as much flavor as possible. Strain the mixture through a wire-mesh strainer, then again through a paper coffee filter. Sweeten to taste, and serve cold as a lemonade-type beverage; or, use the unsweetened liquid in recipes.

For stronger sumac juice, you can reduce it to approximately half-volume by cooking (however, you are eliminating much of the vitamin C by heating it). Or, add more sumac clusters to already prepared sumac juice and repeat the juice-making process to get a stronger liquid.

Caution: People who are highly allergic to poison ivy, mangoes or cashews should avoid all sumacs, which are in the same family and may cause a severe allergic reaction.

Sumac Tea

Sumac makes a pleasant hot tea that is slightly tart, with floral overtones. It's similar to chamomile tea, or to a mild version of the commercial herbal-tea blend called Red Zinger.

4 good-sized sumac clusters, or about 1 cup of picked berries

4 cups water

Honey or sugar to taste, optional

Rinse the sumac clusters briefly, and set aside to drain. Heat water to boiling in saucepan; remove from heat and set aside to cool for about 5 minutes. While water is cooling, cut smaller clusters away from woody stems, discarding stems. Add clusters or picked berries to hot water and let stand for 5 minutes. Use potato masher or large wooden spoon to bruise the sumac; you don't want to crack the seeds doing this, so don't use too much force. Let stand for about 5 minutes longer, then strain through a damp tea towel or several layers of cheesecloth. Serve warm or cold, adding sweetening to taste if you like.

Variation: Sumac-Mint Tea
Add a few fresh mint leaves to the hot water with the sumac.

If you want iced tea, chill the brewed tea for an hour before serving. I like hot sumac tea unsweetened, but you can add sugar or honey to taste if you prefer; iced tea tastes better if sweetened lightly. Iced sumac tea is best the day it is made; it begins to turn an unappetizing brown after a day in the refrigerator.

Cedar-Planked Salmon with Sumac-Maple Glaze

4 to 6 servings

Cooking salmon on cedar planks is traditional in the Pacific Northwest. In this version, the salmon is topped with a tangy-sweet glaze made from sumac juice and maple syrup.

Red cedar plank, about ½ inch thick and large enough to hold fish

1 cup strained sumac juice

1-inch chunk peeled fresh gingerroot

1 clove garlic

2 strips orange zest (colored rind only, with none of the white pith), each about 2 inches long by ½ inch wide

¾ cup pure maple syrup (don't use substitutes in this recipe)

1 tablespoon soy sauce

2 teaspoons butter

2-pound fillet of salmon, skin on

Salt and freshly ground pepper

In a clean bucket, soak plank in water to cover for 8 hours or overnight; weight with clean rocks to keep plank submerged. When you're ready to start cooking, prepare the glaze: In small, heavy-bottomed non-aluminum saucepan, boil sumac juice over high heat until reduced to about ⅓ cup (see "Reducing Liquid," pg. 121). While the sumac juice is cooking, chop the gingerroot, garlic and orange zest until fine in a food processor.

When the sumac juice is reduced, add the chopped gingerroot mixture, the maple syrup and soy sauce. Continue boiling until reduced slightly, about 5 minutes. Remove from heat and stir in butter; set aside until cooled to room temperature. While glaze is cooling, prepare grill for direct, high heat (see "Grilling: Direct vs. Indirect Heat," pg. 151). Drain plank and pat dry. Place salmon on plank, skin-side down; season to taste with salt and pepper. Reserve half of the glaze; brush fish with remaining glaze. Place plank on grill grate directly over heat. Cover grill and cook until fish is just opaque, 15 to 25 minutes depending on the thickness of the fish. (The plank may catch fire around the edges near the end of cooking time; don't worry about it unless it gets too strong. If necessary, douse the edges with a spray bottle of water.) When the salmon is almost done, warm reserved sauce over medium heat, then transfer to a small serving bowl. Serve salmon on plank, or transfer fish to a serving platter; pass warmed sauce with the fish. Discard the plank after use.

 Buy untreated cedar from the lumberyard, or look at a specialty shop or upscale grocer for planks that are marketed specifically for cooking.

Grilling: Direct vs. Indirect Heat

When preparing your charcoal or gas grill, you can set it up for direct or indirect heat. Direct heat works well for foods that need hot, quick cooking; indirect heat is better for those that need longer cooking and would burn if exposed directly to the hottest part of the fire.

For direct cooking with charcoal, pile a good quantity of coals in the center of the grill and light them; when they are covered with ash, spread them out just a bit, and put the food directly over the coals. For direct cooking with gas, light one or more burners and preheat on high; when the grill is hot, place the food directly over the hot burner still set on high.

For indirect cooking with charcoal, pile coals to one side of the grill and light them; when they are covered with ash, spread them out evenly over half of the grill, and put the food over the half of the grill that has no coals. For indirect cooking with gas, light one burner and preheat on high; when the grill is hot, reduce heat slightly and place the food on the grate away from the lit area. Note that some recipes call for browning meat over direct heat, then moving it to the cooler, indirect side to finish cooking.

Other recipes in this book featuring sumac:

Elderberry-Sumac Jelly, pg. 63

THIMBLEBERRIES *(Rubus parviflorus)*

Some wild fruits, such as blueberries and raspberries, have been cultivated and are sold in the supermarket. Thimbleberry is one that you'll probably never see; the fruit is so soft and delicate that it would never stand up to commercial handling. In fact, it's difficult to bring enough home to use for recipes; the fruits are so soft that they get smashed in the berry bucket if you put in more than two or three layers of fruit.

Thimbleberries are easy to identify; look for a waist-high shrub that has maple-like leaves and red fruits that look like flattened raspberries. Don't pick pink fruits; these are underripe and are hard, with a somewhat bitter flavor. Wait until the fruit is rich red and soft. The soft red cap can be pulled off when it's ripe; the white core will remain behind on the plant.

If you can get a whole thimbleberry off the plant intact, you'll understand where the name comes from: the hollow fruit is large enough to put over your finger, like a thimble.

Most foragers eat thimbleberries raw, standing in the patch and eating the fruits as fast as they can pick them. Thimbleberries travel poorly because they're so soft, but you can pack them in flat containers (the kind you might buy a small amount of deli cole-slaw in) and transport them in a cooler. If you do manage to gather enough thimbleberries to make juice, follow the instructions for raspberries on pg. 118.

Thimbleberry Smoothie

2 servings

This is a terrific—yet healthy—breakfast drink.

½ to ¾ cup thimbleberries (3 to 5 ounces)

Half of a banana

¾ cup soy milk or regular whole milk

½ cup plain yogurt (reduced-fat or fat-free works fine)

½ cup ice cubes

1 tablespoon honey, or to taste

¼ teaspoon vanilla extract

Combine all ingredients in blender. Process until smooth. Divide between two glasses; serve immediately.

Variation: Substitute any bramble (raspberries, blackberries or dewberries), soft-seeded berry (blueberries, huckleberries, serviceberries or bilberries), or strawberries for the thimbleberries. Adjust honey as needed, depending on the sweetness of the fruit.

Sautéed Fish with Thimbleberries

2 servings

Here's an elegant use for a handful of fresh thimbleberries.

¾ pound boneless, skinless fillets from a mild fish such as grouper, cod, walleye or halibut

1 tablespoon unsalted butter

1 tablespoon olive oil

¼ cup finely diced red onion

Salt and freshly ground pepper

A small amount of all-purpose flour for dusting fish

3 tablespoons dry sherry

¼ cup Beaujolais or other light, dry but fruity red wine

⅓ cup thimbleberries (about 2 ounces)

2 teaspoons chopped fresh oregano

2 teaspoons chopped fresh chives

2 teaspoons minced fresh parsley

Rinse fish in cold water; pat dry with paper towels and set aside. In skillet that will hold the fish comfortably, melt butter in oil over medium heat. Add onion; sauté until tender-crisp, 3 to 4 minutes. Meanwhile, sprinkle fish with salt and pepper to taste; dust lightly with flour, shaking off excess.

When onion is tender-crisp, add fish fillets to skillet on top of the onions (don't push them to the sides), placing the most attractive side down. Increase heat to medium-high and cook until fish is nicely browned and cooked about halfway through; this will take 3 to 5 minutes, depending on the thickness of your fillets. Turn fillets carefully so the browned side, which will be crusted with onion, is up. Cook for about a minute. Pour sherry around the edges (not on top of the fish); the sherry will cook away almost instantly. Pour red wine around the edges; scatter thimbleberries and herbs around the edges. Cook until wine has reduced and fish is just cooked through; if the fillets are thick, you may need to cover the pan for a few minutes to cook the fish through. Serve fillets topped with thimbleberry mixture spooned over the top.

Substitution: Substitute raspberries, dewberries or blackberries for the thimbleberries.

You may vary the herbs to suit your taste, but don't substitute dried herbs; the dish is best with the bright flavor of fresh herbs.

Thimbleberry Filling

½ teaspoon water

½ teaspoon cornstarch

6 ounces thimbleberries (about 1 cup)

1 tablespoon grated apple

1 tablespoon sugar

In small bowl, blend together water and cornstarch; set aside. In small, heavy-bottomed saucepan, combine thimbleberries, apple and sugar. Crush fruit gently with a potato masher to start juices flowing. Heat to boiling over medium-high heat, then cook, stirring frequently, until mixture is no longer runny; this will take 9 to 11 minutes. Add cornstarch mixture, stirring constantly; cook for about 1 minute longer, or until thick. Cool before using.

Use this to prepare Easy Bear Claws (pg. 20), Fruit-Striped Cookie Fingers (pg. 119), or Fruit-Filled Muffins (pg. 146). Refrigerate extra filling, and use to top oatmeal or toast.

Other recipes in this book featuring thimbleberries:
Fruits of the Forest Pie, pg. 156
Brambleberry Cream Sauce, pg. 157

Quick ideas for using thimbleberries:
Top a small bowl of thimbleberries, mixed with raspberries if you have some, with yogurt, and sprinkle with a little granola. This is a favorite breakfast for campers.
Place some thimbleberries on a toasted, well-buttered English muffin; mash somewhat with a knife and spread the berries over the toast. Sprinkle with just a bit of sugar if you like; eat immediately.
Use thimbleberries in any recipe calling for raspberries, or mix the two in recipes.

WINTERGREEN (CREEPING) and CREEPING SNOWBERRY *(Gaultheria procumbens, G. hispidula)*

These two related plants produce tiny berries; wintergreen berries are red, while those of creeping snowberry are white. Both have a spicy, minty smell and taste, and make a wonderfully refreshing trail nibble. It's hard to gather them in large quantities, but I've read that some foragers gather quantities and make preserves from them.

Leaves of both plants may be used to make tea, which is used to relieve upset stomach. Wintergreen leaves are commonly used in this fashion; in fact, wintergreen is sometimes referred to as "teaberry" because it is so often used to make tea. Leaves of creeping snowberry are much milder, so the tea needs to steep for several hours, while wintergreen tea is ready after about 15 minutes.

Both wintergreen and common snowberry contain methyl salicylate, an aspirin-like compound, in the leaves and fruit. Persons who are sensitive to aspirin should not ingest any part of these plants.

Wintergreen Malt   2 servings

This is a delightful malt, with a clean, refreshing taste. It's a good use for a small harvest of these berries.

2 to 3 heaping scoops vanilla ice cream

1½ cups whole milk, very cold

3 tablespoons malted milk powder

2 to 3 tablespoons creeping snowberry or wintergreen berries

4 vanilla wafers or other sugar wafers, optional

Combine all ingredients except wafers in blender. Cover tightly and pulse on-and-off several times, until ingredients are beginning to mix and have filled the bottom of the blender. Blend on regular setting until desired consistency, 30 to 45 seconds. Divide between 2 chilled malt glasses; tuck 2 wafers into each malt and serve immediately.

Quick ideas for using creeping snowberry and wintergreen berries:
Scatter a few on top of ice cream for a minty sundae.
Mash a handful of berries and add to applesauce.

MIXED BERRY DISHES

Following are two very special recipes that use a mixed bag of wild berries or fruits. Substitutions are given for some of the ingredients, in case you are missing one of the species listed.

Fruits of the Forest Pie

1 pie (6 to 8 servings)

This uses a mixture of brambles and berries—heaven in a pie crust. Use what you have on hand (or in the freezer) to fill the amounts noted. Use crabapples, hawthorns or domestic apples for the apple portion; be sure to remove all seeds and blossom remnants if using crabapples or haws.

Ready-to-use pastry for two-crust pie

1½ cups blueberries, serviceberries, huckleberries or bilberries— all one type, or a mix

1½ cups brambles such as raspberries (red or black), blackberries, thimbleberries or good-quality dewberries—all one type, or a mix

½ cup grated apple, crabapple or hawthorn

¾ to 1 cup sugar, depending on the sweetness of the berries

1 tablespoon cornstarch

1 tablespoon butter, cut into small pieces

Optional wash: 1 egg lightly beaten with 1 tablespoon milk

Heat oven to 400°F. Line pie plate with one crust; set aside. In mixing bowl, combine berries, brambles, apple, sugar and cornstarch; stir gently to combine. Spoon into bottom crust. Scatter cut-up butter over the fruit. Brush crust edges lightly with water; top with second crust, crimping edges to seal (or, make a lattice crust; see "Making a Lattice-Top Pie," pg. 69). Brush crust with egg mixture; cut several slits in crust. Place pie on a baking sheet (to catch drips). Bake for 10 minutes, then reduce heat to 350°F and cook until crust is rich golden brown and filling bubbles through slits, 35 to 45 minutes longer. Cool on wire rack; best served slightly warm, the day it is made.

Substitution: You may use up to ½ cup mountain fly honeysuckle berries in the mix to replace some of the blueberry group; they should be combined with other berries rather than making up the full 1½ cups.

Brambleberry Cream Sauce

About 2 cups (enough for 6 to 8 servings)

Serve this sauce warm with crêpes, over angel food cake or biscuits, on cereal or pancakes, or however you like.

4 tablespoons (half of a stick) cold unsalted butter, divided

2 tablespoons all-purpose flour

1 cup heavy cream

$2/3$ cup sugar

$1/4$ teaspoon salt

**$3/4$ cup red raspberries, thimbleberries or red dewberries—
all one type, or a mix**

**$3/4$ cup black raspberries, blackberries or black dewberries—
all one type, or a mix**

In heavy-bottomed saucepan, melt 2 tablespoons of the butter over medium heat. Whisk in flour. Cook, whisking constantly, until mixture thickens and turns golden; don't let it burn. Whisk in cream, sugar and salt. Cook over medium heat, whisking frequently, until mixture bubbles and thickens to saucelike consistency; this will take 3 or 4 minutes. Stir in berries. Cook, stirring gently a few times, for about a minute. Remove from heat. Quickly cut remaining butter into 4 pieces. Add a piece to the warm sauce and stir until it melts. Repeat with remaining butter, adding just 1 piece at a time and stirring until it melts. Serve immediately, or keep warm until ready to serve.

SIX RECIPES USING WILD FRUIT JUICE or SYRUP

Here are a half-dozen recipes that work well with juice or syrup you've made from just about any type of wild fruit. One or two suggested juices are listed with most recipes, but feel free to experiment, substituting a different type of juice for the one listed. You may need to increase the amount of sweetening if your juice is particularly tart.

Wild Fruit Sorbet
About 3 cups

This basic recipe works with any wild fruit juice in this book, except mountain ash; you need an ice-cream maker to prepare this. Depending on the type of fruit juice you use, your sorbet may be pink, purple, rich purple, greenish or red. For an attractive presentation, place a small scoop of the sorbet in a dish with a small scoop of lemon sherbet and another of vanilla ice cream; garnish with a shortbread or ginger cookie.

1 cup sugar

⅝ cup water

1¾ cups blackberry juice or other wild fruit juice

A pinch of salt

1 egg white (from commercially pasteurized egg if concerned about salmonella)

If using ice-cream maker that requires pre-freezing, place it in freezer as directed by manufacturer, generally 12 to 24 hours. Combine sugar and water in small saucepan. Heat to boiling, stirring just until sugar dissolves. Remove from heat; cool to room temperature, then place in freezer for 30 minutes, or in refrigerator for at least 2 hours, until completely chilled. Combine sugar mixture, wild fruit juice and salt in a 1-quart jar; chill overnight.

Transfer mixture to prepared ice-cream maker and churn until slushy and beginning to hold a soft shape, 7 to 10 minutes. In small bowl, beat egg white with a fork for 45 seconds, then add to ice cream maker with slush. Continue to churn until mixture freezes to a soft ice-cream consistency, 12 to 15 minutes longer. The sorbet will be very soft at this point. Scoop sorbet into plastic container and freeze for at least 3 hours; mixture can be frozen for up to a week. It will remain scoopable for several days; if it becomes too hard to scoop, place container in the refrigerator for about 30 minutes to soften the sorbet slightly before serving.

Wild Fruit Gels (Gumdrops)

This works great with the juice from any wild fruit in this book, except mountain ash. Juice from dark fruits like chokecherries, raspberries or blackberries makes attractive, deeply colored gels; for example, juice from cranberries or highbush cranberries make stunning, bright-red gels. Note: This is based on a recipe that appeared in Family Circle *magazine in the early 1970s. I've cut the recipe in half; if you want to make a full batch, simply double the ingredients and use an 8-inch-square baking dish.*

Half of a 1.75-ounce box powdered pectin (see pg. 164 for information on dividing pectin)

³⁄₈ cup wild fruit juice

¼ teaspoon baking soda

½ cup sugar, plus additional for rolling the gels

½ cup white corn syrup

You'll need two medium saucepans (large, if you're doubling the recipe), two long-handled spoons and a standard-sized loaf pan (glass or nonstick metal work best). Wet the inside of the loaf pan, then line it with plastic wrap, smoothing it out (the water helps hold the wrap in place).

Combine the pectin, fruit juice and baking soda in one pan; combine the ½ cup sugar and the corn syrup in the other. Place a spoon in each pan, and keep those spoons separate from one another throughout the procedure.

Stir both mixtures well, and place both pans over medium-high heat. The pectin mixture will foam up at the beginning; stirring will prevent it from boiling over. Cook both mixtures, stirring alternately, until the foam subsides from the pectin mixture and the sugar mixture is boiling vigorously, about 5 minutes. Pour the pectin mixture in a thin, steady stream into the sugar mixture, stirring constantly. Boil the mixture, stirring constantly, for 1 minute longer. Pour the mixture immediately into the loaf pan. Let stand at room temperature, covered very loosely with a piece of cheesecloth to discourage flies, until completely cool; this will take about 2 hours. (Alternately, you can pour the mixture into tiny molds, if you have them.) Place another piece of plastic wrap on top, pressing it against the surface of the mixture; refrigerate for at least 3 hours and as long as overnight.

Unmold gels onto a cutting board; remove plastic wrap. Cut into 1-inch squares with a sharp knife (dip it in very hot water, then dry off, to make cutting easier). Roll gels in sugar, and arrange in a single layer on a serving plate. Refrigerate or freeze for longer storage, keeping a little space between gels and using waxed paper between layers.

Panna Cotta with Fruit Gel Topping

6 servings

Panna cotta means "cooked cream;" it's an elegant but simple Italian dessert. You'll need 6 small ramekins to prepare this version that is crowned with glistening fruit gel. It's a show-stopper that would be great for a special dinner party.

1 cup sliced strawberries (store-bought berries work fine)

1 cup dark-colored wild fruit juice such as wild cherry

½ to ¾ cup sugar

2 tablespoons cold water

1½ teaspoons unflavored gelatin

<u>Panna cotta</u>:

2 tablespoons cold water

2 teaspoons unflavored gelatin

1 cup half-and-half

½ cup (packed) golden brown sugar

2 cups buttermilk

1 teaspoon vanilla extract

Lightly spray 6 ramekins (1 cup each) with nonstick spray. Arrange in a baking dish that holds them comfortably. Divide strawberries evenly between ramekins; set aside. In small, non-aluminum saucepan, combine juice and ½ cup sugar. Heat the mixture over medium heat, stirring constantly, until sugar dissolves. Cool slightly and taste for sweetness; add additional sugar as needed until the sweetness is the way you like it.

Pour cold water into small bowl. Sprinkle gelatin evenly over water; set aside for 5 minutes. Near the end of the 5 minutes, heat fruit juice mixture over medium-high heat until it is boiling gently. Scrape the gelatin mixture into the fruit juice, stirring vigorously to combine. Boil gently for about a minute, then remove from heat and pour into individual ramekins. Freeze until just set, about 30 minutes; or refrigerate until set, 2 to 3 hours.

When the gel is set, prepare the panna cotta: Pour cold water into small bowl. Sprinkle gelatin evenly over water; set aside for 5 minutes. In medium, non-aluminum saucepan, stir together half-and-half and sugar; heat over medium-high heat, stirring constantly, until sugar dissolves. Scrape the gelatin mixture into the half-and-half, stirring vigorously to combine. Remove from heat and cool to lukewarm, stirring frequently. Stir in buttermilk and vanilla. Pour over set gel; cover entire dish with plastic wrap and refrigerate until firm, about 4 hours; can be prepared up to 2 days in advance.

To serve, run a thin knife around the edge of each ramekin, then hold a ramekin in a shallow pan of very hot water for a few seconds to loosen bottom. Place an individual dessert plate over the ramekin and flip the two over as one, holding together tightly. Gently remove ramekin; repeat with remaining desserts. Serve immediately.

Wild Silk Pie with Cream Cheese Topping
1 pie (8 servings)

This pie is very sweet and rich, so a little goes a long way.

1 purchased shortbread crust or deep graham-cracker crust

1 can (14 ounces) Eagle Brand sweetened condensed milk (reduced-fat works fine)

4 egg yolks

1 whole egg

¾ cup wild fruit syrup, or
  ⅔ cup wild fruit juice mixed with ⅔ cup sugar

2 packages (3 ounces each) cream cheese, softened

½ cup powdered sugar

½ cup sour cream (reduced-fat works fine)

1 teaspoon vanilla extract

Heat oven to 350°F. Bake the crust for 5 minutes. Remove from oven and set aside to cool while you prepare the filling. Reduce oven to 325°F.

In large mixing bowl, combine sweetened condensed milk, egg yolks, whole egg and syrup (or juice/sugar mixture). Beat with electric mixer or sturdy whisk until smooth and completely combined. Place prepared crust onto a baking sheet, and pour in the condensed-milk mixture. Bake in center of oven for about 45 minutes, or until knife inserted in center of pie comes out clean.

While pie is baking, prepare cream cheese topping. In medium mixing bowl, combine cream cheese, powdered sugar, sour cream and vanilla. Beat with electric mixer or wooden spoon until smooth and uniform. When pie filling tests done, remove pie from oven and spread cream cheese mixture evenly over the top, spreading gently with rubber spatula. Return to oven and bake for 10 to 15 minutes longer, or until cream cheese mixture can be touched lightly without sticking. Remove pie from oven and cool completely before covering and placing in refrigerator to chill for several hours. Serve cold.

Cappuccino with Flavor Shot Per serving

Just like at the expensive coffee house! You need an espresso machine to make these, but that piece of equipment is becoming quite common in the well-stocked kitchen.

1 tablespoon black cherry syrup or other wild fruit syrup per serving, or to taste

Cold, fresh milk (skim, lowfat or whole)

Finely ground espresso coffee beans

Prepare the espresso maker, getting it up to temperature and ready to steam. Pour the syrup into a large mug; set it aside while you prepare the milk and coffee. Fill the metal pitcher about half full; clip a milk thermometer inside the pitcher so its tip is just below the surface of the milk. Froth the milk with the steam wand, holding the pitcher so the wand is at an angle with the tip just under the surface of the milk. Steam to a temperature of 150°F. Set aside; the temperature will rise another 5°F while it sits.

Pack a full measure of finely ground espresso into the filter basket and tamp it firmly. Pull a shot into a shot glass or other measure, then pour into the mug; for a double, pull a second shot and add it to the mug. Immediately pour the steamed milk into the cup, holding back the froth with a spoon; fill the mug half to two-thirds full of steamed milk. Spoon the froth over the coffee, filling the mug to the brim.

 Some baristas chill the metal milk pitcher for a few minutes in the freezer to produce better froth. Also, some steam the milk first, then "pull the shot" of espresso; others make the espresso before steaming the milk.

Italian Cremosa Soda Per serving

A cooling beverage that is welcome in hot weather.

3 tablespoons raspberry syrup or other wild fruit syrup

½ cup cold whole milk, or a mix of milk and half-and-half

Crushed ice

Carbonated water

In a tall glass, stir together the syrup and milk. Fill glass half full with crushed ice; add carbonated water to the brim. Serve with a straw, and a tall spoon for mixing.

GENERAL INSTRUCTIONS and INFORMATION

The information that follows applies to a number of fruits in this book. Here you'll find information on making syrup, jelly and jam; dehydrating fruits and making fruit leathers; sterilizing canning jars; and processing in a water-bath canner.

Wild Berry or Fruit Syrup   About 1½ cups syrup per cup of juice

This works great with juice from a variety of wild berries and fruits. Use it as you would use maple syrup: on pancakes, over ice cream, on hot cereal, etc. For a refreshing beverage, pour a few tablespoons of syrup into a glass of sparkling water with ice cubes, or add a bit of syrup to a glass of chilled white wine.

1 cup juice from wild berries or fruit

Sugar as directed in Group lists below

3 tablespoons corn syrup

Group A (use 1 cup sugar per cup of juice): Autumn olives, blackberries, chokecherries, crabapples, currants, dewberries, grapes, hawthorns, mulberries, raspberries, wild cherries.

Group B (use 1¼ cups sugar per cup of juice): Cranberries, elderberries (also add 1 teaspoon lemon juice), gooseberries, plums, rose hips.

Group C (use 1½ cups sugar per cup of juice): Chokeberries, creeping Oregon grape, highbush cranberries.

Prepare jars, bands and lids as directed on pg. 171 (even if you won't be canning the syrup, it's a good idea to sterilize the jars and lids as directed). In medium non-aluminum saucepan, combine juice and sugar. Heat over medium-high heat, stirring constantly, until sugar dissolves and mixture just begins to boil. Adjust heat so mixture boils gently. Add corn syrup and cook, stirring almost constantly, for 5 minutes; watch for boilover and adjust the heat to prevent a too-vigorous boil. After 5 minutes, pour into hot, sterilized jars; seal with new lids and clean bands. To can, process in boiling-water bath for 10 minutes (see pg. 171 for canning instructions). Or, cool and store in the refrigerator.

 *The instructions are for 1 cup of prepared juice; however, you can proportionally increase the ingredients for any amount of juice.*

Jelly Instructions (using pectin)

Pectin is a substance that helps fruit juices set, or jell, when making jelly or jam. Most fruits—wild or domestic—don't have enough natural pectin to set properly, so packaged pectin needs to be added. Packaged pectin comes in two forms: a powder, typically sold in a 1.75-ounce box, and a liquid, typically sold in a box containing two 3-ounce pouches. (In the past, liquid pectin was sold in a larger bottle; the cook had to measure it out for smaller batches.) The packages contain helpful inserts with recipes for common domestic fruits; some of these, such as black raspberries, crabapples and currants, also grow in the wild, so you can use the recipes in the box for those fruits—if you have enough juice. Other wild fruits are not included on the insert, but those that make good jelly have been included in this book. Recipes for jelly are found throughout this book, with individual fruit accounts; the instructions below are general, and apply to all jelly recipes that use packaged pectin.

Recipes that come with packaged pectin are very specific, calling for precise amounts of fruit juice, sugar and pectin, and exact cooking procedures. However, these recipes require a lot of juice—as much as 7 cups, depending on the type of fruit. A box of powdered pectin makes more jelly—and requires more juice—than a pouch of liquid pectin. For example, a batch of currant jelly made with Sure-Jell powdered pectin, prepared according to the recipe in the box, requires 6½ cups of juice and yields 9 cups of jelly; a batch made with Certo liquid pectin requires 5 cups of juice and yields 8 cups of jelly.

Wild fruit juice is not always easy to come by, and you may want to use some of it for other recipes rather than making, say, 10 jars of one type of jelly. Liquid pectin allows you to make a smaller amount, but it still might use more juice than you want. Another option is to divide the pectin to make small-batch jelly; this requires a bit of tinkering.

The most challenging task is dividing the packaged pectin into smaller amounts, and it's important to measure accurately. The best method is to weigh the contents of a full box of pectin on a gram scale (ounce scales are not precise enough), then weigh out the portion you need. For example, the powder in a 1.75-ounce box of Sure-Jell pectin I checked weighs 51 grams, so if a recipe calls for ⅔ of a box, use 34 grams (51 divided by 3 is 17; multiply by 2 to get 34). If you don't have a gram scale, measure the powder very carefully with measuring spoons (scoop or spoon the powder into the measuring spoon until it is completely full and somewhat mounded, then level off the top with the back of a knife), then divide accordingly. The same box of powdered pectin that weighs 51 grams measures 16½ teaspoons (5 tablespoons plus 1½ teaspoons) with my measuring spoons, so ⅔ of a box would be 11 teaspoons (16.5 divided by 3 is 5.5; multiply by 2 to get 11).

Small-batch jelly also cooks slightly differently than large-batch jelly, such as those on the insert in the pectin box; the smaller batch loses proportionally more liquid due to evaporation than a larger batch. If you're experimenting with your own small-batch recipes, you'll need to add just a bit more liquid than what would be indicated by simply dividing a full-batch recipe. Standard recipes also account for varying amounts of natural pectin that is in specific fruits, and so use varying amounts of juice in proportion to the added pectin depending on the type of fruit. Wild fruits vary quite a bit in natural pectin content, especially if they're not fully ripe. And some jellies take a week or even longer to set up—wild cherry is one I've had this experience with.

In summary, when working with wild fruits, you may occasionally end up with jelly that doesn't set, or jelly that is too firm. If the jelly is still liquid-like 10 days after processing, use it like syrup; it will be delicious. If the jelly is too solid, you can melt it and stir in a little water before using. Another option for too-firm jelly (or jam) is to serve it as "cheese." Set the jar in a pan of very hot water for a few minutes, then slide the jelly out onto a plate. Slice it, and serve it on its own, or use the slices to top toast that's been smeared with cream cheese. Gooseberries are often prepared as "cheese" in England and served in this fashion. It's a delicious solution for jelly or jam that is too thick to spread.

How to cook jelly with added pectin

Prepare half-pint canning jars, bands and lids as described on pg. 171. Measure the sugar you'll need, and set it aside so it is ready to use. Combine juice, and lemon juice if listed, in a non-aluminum saucepan or pot that holds at least four times the amount of juice you're using. Whisk in powdered pectin until dissolved; add butter if using (it helps reduce foaming). Heat to boiling over high heat, stirring frequently. When mixture comes to a full, rolling boil that can't be stirred down, add the sugar. Cook, stirring constantly, until the mixture again comes to a full, foaming boil. Boil for 1 minute, stirring constantly (if mixture threatens to boil over, move from heat for a few seconds, then reduce heat slightly and return pan to heat). Remove from heat, and stir for a minute or 2 to settle the foam; if there is still foam on top, skim with a clean spoon and discard. Pour into prepared jars, leaving ¼ inch headspace; seal with prepared lids and bands. Process in boiling-water bath for 10 minutes (see pg. 171), or cool and store in refrigerator.

Here are recipes for specific wild-fruit jellies:

Autumn olive, pg. 10
Blackberry or dewberry, pg. 14
Chokeberry or aronia, pg. 38
Cranberry, pg. 50
Creeping Oregon grape, pg. 53
Currant, pg. 56
Elderberry, pg. 63
Gooseberry, pg. 71
Grape, pg. 76
Hawthorn, pg. 88
Highbush cranberry, pg. 93
Mountain ash, pg. 98, 101
Mulberry, pg. 103
Plums (American wild plum, beach plum), pg. 115
Raspberry (red or black) or dewberry, pg. 124
Rose hip, pg. 127
Wild cherries (pin cherry, black cherry, sand cherry, chokecherry), pg. 33

Jelly Instructions for Fruits with Natural Pectin

Some fruit juices, such as apple juice, have enough natural pectin that they will set without the addition of commercial pectin. However, natural pectin content varies depending on the ripeness of the fruit, time of year and other conditions, so exact cooking times can't be given; the times listed in individual recipes are a general guideline. There are three ways to test for doneness; here are directions for all three. Use whichever you prefer; you may even want to use two tests on a batch of jelly until you gain experience in jelly-making.

The temperature method is the most scientific test to judge doneness. At 8°F above the boiling point of water, the sugar concentration is high enough that the liquid should jell when it cools; once your mixture reaches that point, it's done. The temperature method works well, but it can be difficult to get a reading. Candy or deep-fat thermometers can be clipped to the side of the pan and monitored throughout cooking, but most need to be immersed into an inch (or more) of boiling liquid to read properly, and that's difficult with a small batch of jelly. Instant-read thermometers require less immersion, but they can't be left in place for more than a few minutes. You can hold them with a tongs and put the tip into the mixture, but it's steamy work because, in spite of the name, these thermometers don't really read "instantly;" it can take up to two minutes.

The temperature method also requires a bit of testing before you start cooking the jelly. We think of 212°F as the "boiling point" of water, but in fact, water boils at different temperatures depending on altitude; even at the same altitude, the boiling temperature may change from day to day depending on atmospheric conditions. Just before you make a batch of jelly, test the boiling temperature on that day, with your particular thermometer (these vary, too; if you test two at the same time, one may show boiling at 212°F, while another shows boiling at, say, 216°F). Add 8 to the boiling temperature shown on your thermometer that day, then cook your jelly to that temperature (so if your thermometer reads 213°F for a pan of boiling water, cook your jelly to 221°F).

The spoon test is also called the sheeting test. To use this method, dip a clean, cool metal spoon into the jelly kettle to spoon up a bit of the mixture. Quickly raise it a foot above the jelly kettle, out of the steam, and turn it sideways so the mixture drips back into the kettle off the side of the spoon. If the mixture forms two large drips that flow together and fall off the spoon in a sheet, it is done; get it off the heat immediately. Sometimes, your range hood gets in the way of this test; and, you need a supply of clean, cool spoons in case you need to test the jelly several times.

The cold-plate test is foolproof and easy to use, but sometimes, it's hard to know when to start testing. Many cooks use the spoon test as a preliminary, and follow up with the cold-plate test to confirm doneness. To use the cold-plate test, place a ceramic plate in the freezer to chill when you start boiling the jelly mixture. When you think the jelly is approaching doneness, drop a teaspoon of the mixture onto the cold plate and return it to the freezer for about a minute. Remove the plate from the freezer, and push at the jelly with your fingertip. If the surface wrinkles and the jelly seems firm, with no weeping around the edge, the jelly is done; get it off the heat immediately. If it is not done, return the plate to the freezer and continue cooking the jelly, testing again in a few minutes.

Jam Instructions (using pectin)

Making jam with added pectin is similar to making pectin-added jelly, but you start with puréed or crushed fruit rather than juice. For small-batch jam, you'll need to divide the pectin as instructed in the jelly instructions on pg. 164.

Prepare half-pint canning jars, bands and lids as described on pg. 171. Measure the sugar you'll need, and set it aside so it is ready to use. Combine puréed or crushed fruit, and lemon juice if listed, in a non-aluminum saucepan or pot that holds at least four times the amount of purée or crushed fruit you're using. Whisk in powdered pectin until dissolved; add butter if using (it helps reduce foaming). Heat to boiling over high heat, stirring frequently. When mixture comes to a full, rolling boil that can't be stirred down, add the sugar. Cook, stirring constantly, until the mixture again comes to a full, foaming boil. Boil for 1 minute, stirring constantly; if mixture threatens to boil over, move from heat for a few seconds, then reduce heat slightly and return pan to heat before it stops boiling. Remove from heat, and stir for a minute or 2 to settle the foam; if there is still foam on top, skim with a clean spoon and discard. Pour into prepared jars, leaving ¼ inch headspace; seal with prepared lids and bands. Process in boiling-water bath for 10 minutes (see pg. 171), or cool and store in refrigerator.

Here are recipes for specific wild-fruit jams using pectin:
Autumn olive, pg. 10
Blackberry, pg. 17

Dehydrating Wild Berries and Fruits

Home drying, or dehydrating, is an excellent preservation method for many wild fruits. It works on a simple principle: warm air is circulated over prepared foods to remove the moisture. Food is generally held on a tray that allows maximum air flow. A number of home dehydrators are available; your oven can also be pressed into service. Dehydrators come with their own trays. For oven dehydrating, stretch a piece of bridal-veil netting over a cake-cooling rack, then secure it to the rack with twist-ties. Fruit leathers, by the way, need to be dried on a solid liner sheet (dehydrator) or plastic-lined baking sheet (oven); see pg. 170 for information on fruit leathers.

Fruits can generally be dried with no preparation other than washing and perhaps slicing. (In comparison, vegetables generally need to be blanched, or par-boiled, before dehydrating.) As a general rule, if a fruit can be frozen with no special preparation, it can also be dried with no special preparation. Some fruits dehydrate better if they are first syrup-blanched; the dried fruit will be softer and stickier than untreated fruit, and will have more vibrant color. To prepare the syrup, combine 1 cup sugar and 1 cup white corn syrup with 2 cups water. Heat to boiling, stirring until sugar dissolves. Add fruit; reduce heat and simmer for 5 minutes. Drain and rinse fruit in cold water before drying.

Arrange foods on the trays in even layers, ideally with air space between each piece. However, keep in mind that the food will shrink as it dries, so the spaces between the foods will grow. Stir or rearrange the food periodically during drying, to separate pieces that may be stuck together and to promote even drying.

Quality home dehydrators have thermostats; in general, 145°F is a good temperature for fruits. If you're drying in the oven, set it to the lowest setting possible, and prop the door slightly ajar with a ball of foil or an empty can; this allows moisture to escape, and also keeps the temperature down.

To check foods for dryness, remove a piece or two from the dehydrator or oven, and cool to room temperature before judging doneness. (If you're making fruit leather, remove the entire tray and let it cool slightly before checking.) Some individual pieces may be dry sooner than others; simply remove them from the trays and continue drying the rest until everything is finished. Let the food stand at room temperature for an hour or so, then pack into clean glass jars, seal tightly and store in a cool, dark location. Check it several times over the next few days to be sure that moisture isn't developing inside the jars; if you see any moisture, take the food out and dry it some more in the dehydrator or oven. Properly dehydrated foods retain their quality and freshness for a year or longer. If you notice any mold, however, discard the entire contents of the jar without tasting; moisture has gotten in somehow and compromised the food, and it is no longer safe.

Note: The information here comes largely from my books, *Abundantly Wild: Collecting and Cooking Wild Edibles in the Upper Midwest*, and *The Back-Country Kitchen: Camp Cooking for Canoeists, Hikers and Anglers*.

Blueberries: Frozen or fresh blueberries both dry well, and require no pretreatment; fresh blueberries can be dipped briefly into boiling water to "check" (break) the skin, which reduces drying time. Doneness test: Hard, dark, wrinkled; frozen and "checked" blueberries will be slightly flattened when dry. Drying time: 6 to 8 hours.

Crabapple wedges: Crabapples can be dried with no additional preparation, or syrup-blanched first. To prepare either blanched or unblanched crabapples, quarter washed fruit, removing seeds and blossom end. Syrup-blanch for 5 minutes if you like. Doneness test: The blanched crabapples will be glossy and slightly sticky, with dark-red peels and pinkish flesh; they are rather like a leathery candy. Unblanched crabapples are dry and leathery and have a duller appearance, with tan flesh and brick-red skins. Drying time: 4 to 5½ hours, depending on size of crabapples.

Cranberries: Frozen or fresh cranberries both dry well; those which have been frozen dry a bit more quickly. Blanch in boiling water for about a minute, or until the skins split. Drain and allow to drip dry before spreading on racks. Doneness test: Shrunken, wrinkled, leathery, dark red. Drying time: 6 to 10 hours.

Currants or gooseberries: Frozen or fresh berries both dry well, and require no pre-treatment; fresh berries can be dipped briefly into boiling water to "check" (break) the skin, which reduces drying time. Don't dry prickly gooseberries; the prickles become stiffer, making them very unpleasant to eat. Doneness test: Hard, dark, wrinkled; frozen and "checked" berries will be slightly flattened when dry. Drying time: 8 to 10 hours.

Elderberries: Spread washed elderberries (stemlets removed) on mesh liners over drying trays (elderberries get quite small when dried, and will fall through normal dryer trays). Doneness test: Shrunken and hard. Drying time: 4 to 5 hours.

Ground cherries: Frozen or fresh ground cherries both dry well. Wash and cut into halves; arrange, cut-side up, on dryer trays. Doneness test: They will shrink and flatten quite a bit, becoming leathery; color will deepen. Drying time: About 5 hours.

Mountain ash berries: These mealy berries dry well at room temperature; simply spread them on baking sheets and let stand at room temperature until dry, stirring several times a day. To hasten drying, spread individual berries, or even small berry clusters, on the tray of a food dehydrator or baking sheet for oven drying. Doneness test: Leathery and hard, deep brick color. Drying time (dehydrator or oven): 3 to 4 hours.

Mulberries or raspberries: Spread in single layer on solid liner sheets or baking sheets (for oven drying) to catch drips; no pretreatment is needed. If you like, transfer fruits to regular (ventilated) dryer trays after an hour or 2, after any juices have been released, to hasten drying. Doneness test: Leathery and shrunken. Drying time: 4 to 10 hours; raspberries dry more quickly than mulberries.

Plums: Halve plums and remove pit. Plums can be dried with no further pretreatment, or syrup-blanched first. Arrange plum halves, blanched or not, cut-side up, on dryer trays. Doneness test: Shrunken, firm and leathery; blanched plums will be softer and stickier when dry, while untreated fruit will be harder and more chewy. Drying time: 8 to 24 hours, depending on size of fruit.

Serviceberries: Remove stem and blossom ends. Cut fruits in half for quicker drying, or dry whole. Arrange in single layer on trays. Doneness test: Shrunken and leathery. Drying time: 6 to 10 hours.

Strawberries: Wash and remove cap. Arrange on dryer trays no more than 2 deep. Doneness test: Leathery and somewhat spongy. Drying time: 4 to 8 hours, depending on size.

Wild Berry or Fruit Leather

Almost any fruit can be dried into a leather; generally, all you need to do is simply purée the fruit in a blender or food processor, sweeten to taste as needed, and dry in a food dehydrator or low oven. (Please read the general information on dehydrating foods on pg. 168.) Hard fruits, such as apples and pears, should be cooked in a little water with a few drops of lemon juice before puréeing; soft berries can be puréed and dried with no cooking.

The purée to be dried into a leather should be fairly thick—a consistency like applesauce works well. If you try to dry a purée that is too thin or watery, the leather will take forever to dry, and may be brittle once dry. If the fruit you're working with is watery, or the purée too runny, cook it down for a bit to thicken it before spreading on the drying sheets.

You can add spices to your purées to vary the flavor; try cinnamon or nutmeg with apple or plum purée, or a bit of orange extract with berry purée. For additional interest, sprinkle the purée before drying with finely chopped nuts, shredded coconut or granola.

Commercial dryers come with solid liner sheets that work well, but I've found that some of them need to be sprayed with nonstick spray, especially if the fruit is extremely sticky. Experiment with a small batch of purée to see how your liner sheets perform. If you're drying in the oven or in a homemade dryer, line rimmed baking sheets with plastic wrap, then tape the wrap to the rims of the baking sheets to keep it in place during filling and drying. One standard-sized sheet will hold about 2 cups of purée.

Pour the purée onto prepared baking sheets or dehydrator liners. Tilt the sheets to evenly distribute the purée; it should be about ¼ inch deep. Dry at 130°-150°F until leathery with no sticky spots; peel from the sheets and flip once during drying if the bottom is not drying properly. Total drying time is generally 4 to 10 hours, but this may vary depending on your equipment, the purée and the weather. If you've used baking sheets lined with plastic wrap, the leather can be peeled off any time; if you've used solid liner sheets with a dehydrator, peel off the leather while it is still warm. Roll up all leathers, and wrap in plastic wrap. They keep well at cool room temperature if properly dried; for long-term storage, wrap the plastic-wrapped rolls in freezer wrap and store in the freezer.

Sterilizing Jars and Canning

Jars and lids used for canning need to be sterilized before filling. It's also a good idea to sterilize jars for jams and jellies even if you plan to store the finished product in the refrigerator or freezer. Modern canning jars have two-piece tops: a flat lid, and a screw-on band. When you're canning, always start with a brand-new lid; the rubber seal won't work if the lid has been used before. Bands can be re-used a number of times, but if they start to get corroded, get rid of them and buy new bands.

Always use jars specially made for canning. These jars can be re-used many times, unless they develop a nick or crack. Inspect each jar by holding it up to the light, looking for cracks or fractures. Then, when you are washing the jar prior to sterilizing it, run your wet finger over the top rim of the jar, checking for nicks. Even a small nick will cause canning failure; if you find jars like this in your collection, pack them up for recycling.

The recipes in this book call for half-pint jars. These are small enough to fit in a large pot such as a Dutch oven, so you don't have to use a full-sized water bath canner. The jars shouldn't sit directly on the bottom of the pot because they might crack from the heat. If you have a rack or a pasta-cooking insert for your pot, use that to raise the jars above the bottom; otherwise, line the bottom of the pot with a clean, thick towel.

Jelly and jam should be poured into the jars the minute they are done cooking, so the jars must be sterilized and ready to go before you start cooking. Wash jars, bands and lids in hot, soapy water, inspecting the rim; rinse well. Place jars on the rack in the pot, then add water to cover them by an inch. Heat to boiling over high heat. Boil the jars for 10 minutes, then turn off the heat and let the jars sit in the hot water until you're ready to fill them. Meanwhile, place washed lids and bands in a saucepan; cover with water. Heat to a vigorous simmer. Cover and remove from heat.

When the jelly or jam is ready, use canning tongs to remove one jar from the pot, pouring its water back into the pot. Fill the jar with food, leaving the amount of head space indicated in the recipe ("head space" is the empty area at the top of the jar). Wipe the jar rim and threads with a clean paper towel. Place a hot lid and band on top, and screw the band on so it is just finger-tight. If you will be canning the food, return the jar to the pot and repeat with remaining food; otherwise, place the filled jar on a rack to cool.

How to process food in a hot-water bath
Once the jars are filled and returned to the pot, add additional hot water if necessary to cover the jars by 1 inch. Heat to boiling over high heat, then begin timing and boil for the amount of time indicated in the recipe. Use canning tongs to remove the jars from the pot, grasping them below the bands (if you grasp the band itself, you could break the seal). Place jars on a thick towel, away from drafts, to cool. When cool, check each jar for a proper seal. The center of the lid should be depressed, and it should not move up and down when pressed with a finger. If any jars are improperly sealed, refrigerate and enjoy as you would any opened jelly or jam. Sealed jars can be stored in a cool, dark place for up to a year.

INDEX

A

Aluminum cookware, about, 58
American wild plums, *see:* Plums
Applesauce, Easy Cherry, 37
Aronia Jelly, 38
Aronia, *see:* Chokeberries or aronia
Asian-Inspired Plum Sauce, 113
Autumn olive, 6-10
    Autumn Olive "Berries" for Baking, 8
    Autumn Olive Jam, 10
    Autumn Olive Jelly, 10
    autumn olive syrup, 163
    Cookies with Dried Fruit, Nuts and
      White Chocolate Chips, 28
    making juice or purée, 6
    Refrigerator Cookies with Autumn
      Olive "Berries", 9
    Six Recipes Using Wild Fruit Juice or
      Syrup, 158–162
    Sweet Autumn Olive Bread, 7

B

Baked desserts,
    Blackberry-Apple Crisp, 15
    Blueberry Jalousie, 22
    Individual Currant Cheesecakes, 57
    Mulbery Ripple Cheesecake, 104
    Raspberry Shortcakes, 123
    Rice Pudding with Wild Berries, 107
    Spicy Gooseberry-Apple Crisp, 74
    see also: Cakes, Cookies, Pies
Beach plums, *see:* Plums
Beverages,
    Blackberry Sidecar, 13
    Cappuccino with Flavor Shot, 162
    Crabapplejack, 44
    Currant Cordial, 61
    Elderberry Liqueur, 65
    Highbush Sunrise, 91
    Homemade Cherry Cordial, 34
    Italian Cremosa Soda, 162
    sumac-ade, 148
    Sumac Tea, 149
    Thimbleberry Smoothie, 152
    Wild Cherry-Lemonade Sparkler, 35
    Wintergreen Malt, 155
Bilberries, *see:* Blueberries, bilberries and
    huckleberries
Blackberries and black dewberries,
    11-17
    Blackberry-Apple Crisp, 15
    Blackberry Filling, 14
    Blackberry Freezer Jam, 16
    Blackberry Jelly, 14
    Blackberry Sidecar, 13
    blackberry syrup, 163

Blackberry Turnovers, 12
Brambleberry Cream Sauce, 157
Easy Bear Claws, 20
Fruit-Filled Muffins, 146
Fruits of the Forest Pie, 156
Fruit-Striped Cookie Fingers, 119
making juice or purée, 11
Mulberry Ripple Cheesecake, 104
Rice Pudding with Wild Berries, 107
Sautéed Fish with Thimbleberries, 153
Six Recipes Using Wild Fruit Juice or
    Syrup, 158–162
Smooth Blackberry Sauce, 12
Smoother Blackberry Jam, 17
Thimbleberry Smoothie, 152
Wild Berry Vinegar, 13
Wild Fruit Gels (Gumdrops), 159
Black cherries, *see:* Wild cherries
Blackhaws, *see:* Nannyberries, withe-rod
    and blackhaws
Black raspberries, *see:* Raspberries
**Blueberries, bilberries and huckle-
    berries**, 18-29
    Blackberry-Apple Crisp, 15
    Blueberry Filling, 23
    Blueberry Jalousie, 22
    Blueberry-Maple Breakfast Casserole, 29
    Blueberry Spirals with Cardamom, 25
    Blueberry Streusel Muffins, 21
    Classic Blueberry Pie, 19
    Colorful Fruit Salad, 30
    Cookies with Dried Fruit, Nuts and
      White Chocolate Chips, 28
    dehydrating, 169
    Easy Bear Claws, 20
    Fruit-Filled Muffins, 146
    Fruits of the Forest Pie, 156
    Fruit-Striped Cookie Fingers, 119
    Gravel Pie with Dried Blueberries, 26
    Individual Currant Cheesecakes, 57
    Old-Fashioned Blueberry Dumplings, 27
    Overnight Multi-Grain Cereal with
      Fruit and Nuts, 59
    Refrigerator Cookies with Dried
      Berries, 9
    Serviceberry or Blueberry Freezer
      Jam, 134
    Serviceberry Pudding Cake, 138
    Thimbleberry Smoothie, 152
    Wild Blueberry Pancakes, 24
Blue Cheese and Red Currant Butter, 56
Brambleberry Cream Sauce, 157
Breads, *see:* Muffins, Quick breads
Breakfast and brunch dishes,
    Blueberry-Maple Breakfast Casserole, 29
    Camper's Delight Breakfast, 122
    Chokeberry-Cornmeal Cake, 39

Hawthorn and Sausage Brunch
    Casserole, 87
Microwave Oatmeal with Serviceberries
    and Nuts, 139
Old-Fashioned Blueberry Dumplings, 27
Overnight Multi-Grain Cereal with
    Fruit and Nuts, 59
Serviceberry and Ricotta Brunch Ring,
    135
Thimbleberry Smoothie, 152
Wild Blueberry Pancakes, 24
see also: Muffins, Quick breads,
    Sweet rolls
Bunchberries, 30
    Colorful Fruit Salad, 30
Butter, salted vs. unsalted, 55

C

Cabbage, Red, with Juniper and Bacon, 97
Cakes,
    Chokeberry-Cornmeal Cake, 39
    Gooseberry Pudding Cake, 73
    Highbush Cranberry Spice Cake, 90
    Nannyberry Carrot Cake, 110
    Serviceberry Pudding Cake, 138
Camper's Delight Breakfast, 122
Canning instructions, 171
Cappuccino with Flavor Shot, 162
Carrot Cake, Nannyberry, 110
Cedar-Planked Salmon with Sumac-Maple
    Glaze, 150
Cheesecake, Mulberry Ripple, 104
Cheesecakes, Individual Currant, 57
Cherries, *see:* Wild cherries
Cherry Barbecue Sauce, 36
Cherry Wigglers, 33
Chicken Salad with Ground Cherries and
    Almonds, 80
Chicken with Wild Raspberry Sauce, 120
Chokeberries or aronia, 38-41
    Aronia Jelly, 38
    Chokeberry-Cornmeal Cake, 39
    chokeberry syrup, 163
    making purée or juice, 38
    Pear and Chokeberry Mincemeat
      and Pie, 40-41
    Six Recipes Using Wild Fruit Juice or
      Syrup, 158–162
Chokecherries, *see:* Wild cherries
Citrus fruits, zesting, 34
Classic Blueberry Pie, 19
Coarse Russian Olive Mustard, 131
Colorful Fruit Salad, 30
Cookies,
    Cookies with Dried Fruit, Nuts and
      White Chocolate Chips, 28

Fruit-Striped Cookie Fingers, 119
Ground Cherry Custard Bars, 79
Mulberry Thumbprint Cookies, 103
Pillow Cookies with Hackberry Filling, 84
Plum-Dandy Oatmeal Squares, 114
Refrigerator Cookies with Autumn
  Olive "Berries" or Dried Berries, 9
rotating cookies while baking, 9
Cordial, Currant, 61
Cordial, Homemade Cherry, 34
Crabapples, 42-46
  "Berries" for Baking, 8
  Crabapple Filling, 45
  Crabapple-Ginger-Cardamom Jam, 46
  Crabapplejack, 44
  Crabapple Jelly, 43
  crabapple syrup, 163
  dehydrating, 169
  Easy Bear Claws, 20
  Easy Cherry Applesauce, 37
  Fruit-Filled Muffins, 146
  Fruits of the Forest Pie, 156
  Fruit-Striped Cookie Fingers, 119
  Hawthorn and Sausage Brunch
    Casserole, 87
  Highbush-Apple Leather, 94
  making juice, 42
  Rose Hip-Apple Jelly, 128
  Six Recipes Using Wild Fruit Juice or
    Syrup, 158–162
Cranberries, 47-52
  Cranberry Bread, 51
  Cranberry Jelly, 50
  cranberry syrup, 163
  dehydrating, 169
  Fresh Cranberry Relish, 52
  making juice, 47
  Oatmeal Muffins with Russian
    Olive, 132
  Overnight Multi-Grain Cereal with
    Fruit and Nuts, 59
  Pear and Chokeberry Mincemeat, 40
  Six Recipes Using Wild Fruit Juice or
    Syrup, 158–162
  Spicy Gooseberry-Apple Crisp, 74
  Turkey Breast with Cranberry Pan
    Sauce, 48
  Wild Rice with Cranberries and Nuts, 49
Cream Cheese Frosting, 91
Creeping Oregon grape, 53
  Oregon Grape jelly, 53
  Oregon grape syrup, 163
  Six Recipes Using Wild Fruit Juice or
    Syrup, 158–162
Creeping snowberry, see: Wintergreen
  (creeping) and creeping snowberry
Creeping wintergreen, see: Wintergreen
  (creeping) and creeping snowberry

Crisp, Blackberry-Apple, 15
Currants, 54-61
  Currant-Basil Sauce, 55
  Currant Cordial, 61
  Currant Jelly, 56
  currant syrup, 163
  dehydrating, 169
  Individual Currant Cheesecakes, 57
  making juice, 54
  Overnight Multi-Grain Cereal with Fruit
    and Nuts, 59
  Pears Poached in Spiced Currant
    Juice, 58
  Pumpkin Tart with Currant Glaze, 60
  Red Currant and Blue Cheese Butter, 56
  Six Recipes Using Wild Fruit Juice or
    Syrup, 158–162
Curried Sweet Potato Soup with HBC
  Garnish, 92
Custard Bars, Ground Cherry, 79

D
Dehydrating, 168-170
  Autumn Olive "Berries" for Baking, 8
Dewberries, see: Blackberries and black
  dewberries, Raspberries
Double boiler, improvising, 26
Dumplings, Old-Fashioned Blueberry, 27

E
Easy Bear Claws, 20
Easy Cherry Applesauce, 37
Eggs, substitutes and size, 28
Elderberries, common, 62-67
  dehydrating, 169
  Elderberry Jelly, 63
  Elderberry Liqueur, 65
  Elderberry Meringue Pie, 66
  elderberry syrup, 163
  Fruit Terrine with Elderberry Gel, 64
  making juice, 62
  Pumpkin Tart with Currant Glaze, 60
  Six Recipes Using Wild Fruit Juice or
    Syrup, 158–162
  Wild Berry Vinegar, 13

F
Fish dishes,
  Cedar-Planked Salmon with Sumac-
    Maple Glaze, 150
  Marlin with Rose Hip Glaze, 127
  Sautéed Fish with Thimbleberries, 153
Fragrant sumac, see: Sumac
Freezer jam and jelly,
  blackberry jam, 16
  grape jelly, 77

serviceberry or blueberry jam, 134
  strawberry jam, 142-143
Fresh Cranberry Relish, 52
Fruit-Filled Muffins, 146
Fruits of the Forest Pie, 156
Fruit-Striped Cookie Fingers, 119
Fruit Terrine with Elderberry Gel, 64

G
Gooseberries, 68-75
  dehydrating, 169
  Easy Bear Claws, 20
  Fruit-Filled Muffins, 146
  Fruit-Striped Cookie Fingers, 119
  Gooseberry Bread with Crumble
    Topping, 72
  Gooseberry Pie with Green
    Gooseberries, 69
  Gooseberry Pudding Cake, 73
  gooseberry syrup, 163
  Green Gooseberry Filling, 71
  Green Gooseberry Jam, 70
  Individual Currant Cheesecakes, 57
  making juice, 68
  Ripe Gooseberry Jelly, 71
  Six Recipes Using Wild Fruit Juice or
    Syrup, 158–162
  Spicy Gooseberry-Apple Crisp, 74
  Strawberry-Gooseberry Dessert
    Sauce, 75
Grapes, 76-77
  Grape Jelly, 76, 77
  grape syrup, 163
  Six Recipes Using Wild Fruit Juice or
    Syrup, 158–162
Grill set-up and tips, 151
Gravel Pie with Dried Blueberries, 26
Green Gooseberry Filling, 71
Green Gooseberry Jam, 70
Green Gooseberry Pie, 69
Ground cherries, 78-83
  Chicken Salad with Ground Cherries
    and Almonds, 80
  dehydrating, 169
  Easy Bear Claws, 20
  Fruit-Filled Muffins, 146
  Fruit-Striped Cookie Fingers, 119
  Ground Cherry Custard Bars, 79
  Ground Cherry Filling, 82
  Ground Cherry Jam, 82
  Ground Cherry Pie with Cracker
    Topping, 81
  Sweet and Snappy Ground Cherry
    Salsa, 83
Guelder rose, 89, 93
Gumdrops (Wild Fruit Gels), 159

H

Hackberries, 84-85
Pillow Cookies with Hackberry Filling, 84
Ham Slice with Piquant Plum Sauce, 116
Hawthorns, 86-88
Fruits of the Forest Pie, 156
Hawthorn and Sausage Brunch
Casserole, 87
Hawthorn Jelly, 88
hawthorn syrup, 163
making juice, 86
Six Recipes Using Wild Fruit Juice or
Syrup, 158–162
Highbush cranberries, 89-96
"Berries" for Baking, 8
Curried Sweet Potato Soup with HBC
Garnish, 92
Elderberry Meringue Pie, 66
Highbush-Apple Leather, 94
Highbush Cranberry Jam, 93
Highbush Cranberry Jelly, 93
Highbush Cranberry Sorbet, 95
Highbush Cranberry Spice Cake, 90
highbush cranberry syrup, 163
Highbush Peach Relish, 96
Highbush Sunrise, 91
making juice or purée, 89
Six Recipes Using Wild Fruit Juice or
Syrup, 158–162
Wild Berry Vinegar, 13
Homemade Cherry Cordial, 34
Huckleberries, *see:* Blueberries, bilberries
and huckleberries

I

Individual Currant Cheesecakes, 57
Italian Cremosa Soda, 162

J

Jam instructions (using pectin), 167
Jelly instructions,
for fruits with natural pectin, 166-167
using pectin, 164-165
Jerk Marinade, 140
Juniper, common, 97
Red Cabbage with Juniper and Bacon, 97
Tart Mountain Ash Jelly, 101
Venison Roast with Mountain Ash and
Juniper Rub, 100

L

Lattice-top pie crust, instructions, 69
Leathers, Wild Berry or Fruit, 170
Highbush-Apple Leather, 94
Liqueur, Elderberry, 65

M

Mahonia, *see:* Creeping Oregon grape
Malt, Wintergreen, 155

Marlin with Rose Hip Glaze, 127
Microwave Oatmeal with Serviceberries and
Nuts, 139
Mixed Greens with Strawberries, Honey
Pecans and Blue Cheese, 144
Mountain ash, 98-101
dehydrating, 169
making juice, 98
Pork (or Venison) Chops Glazed with
Mountain Ash, 99
Sweet Mountain Ash Jelly, 98
Tart Mountain Ash Jelly, 101
Venison Roast with Mountain Ash and
Juniper Rub, 100
Mountain fly honeysuckle, 18, 156
Mulberries, 102-107
dehydrating, 169
Easy Bear Claws, 20
Fruit-Filled Muffins, 146
Fruit-Striped Cookie Fingers, 119
making juice or pulp, 102
Mulberry Filling, 105
Mulberry Jelly, 103
Mulberry-Rhubarb Pie with Crumble
Topping, 106
Mulberry Ripple Cheesecake, 104
mulberry syrup, 163
Mulberry Thumbprint Cookies, 103
Rice Pudding with Wild Berries, 107
Six Recipes Using Wild Fruit Juice or
Syrup, 158–162
Muffins,
Blueberry Streusel Muffins, 21
Oatmeal Muffins with Russian
Olive, 132
Serviceberry and Wild Rice Muffins, 136
Mustard, Coarse Russian Olive, 131

N

**Nannyberries, withe-rod and
blackhaws**, 108-111
"Berries" for Baking, 8
Easy Bear Claws, 20
Fruit-Filled Muffins, 146
Fruit-Striped Cookie Fingers, 119
making purée, 108
Nannyberry Barbecue Sauce, 109
Nannyberry Carrot Cake, 110
Nannyberry Filling, 111
Pork Loin Chops with Nannyberry
Barbecue Sauce, 109
No-Cook Grape Jelly, 77

O

Oatmeal Muffins with Russian Olive, 132
Old-Fashioned Blueberry Dumplings, 27
Oregon Grape, *see:* Creeping Oregon
grape
Overnight Multi-Grain Cereal with Fruit
and Nuts, 59

P

Pancakes, Wild Blueberry, 24
Panna Cotta with Fruit Gel Topping, 160
Pectin, dividing powdered, 164
Pear and Chokeberry Mincemeat and Pie,
40-41
Pears Poached in Spiced Currant Juice, 58
Pies,
blind baking pie crusts, 67
Classic Blueberry Pie, 19
Elderberry Meringue Pie, 66
Fruits of the Forest Pie, 156
Gooseberry Pie with Green
Gooseberries, 69
Gravel Pie with Dried Blueberries, 26
Ground Cherry Pie with Cracker
Topping, 81
lattice-top pie instructions, 69
Mulberry-Rhubarb Pie with Crumble
Topping, 106
Pear and Chokeberry Mincemeat Pie, 41
Pumpkin Tart with Currant Glaze, 60
Rustic Black Raspberry Tart, 124
Sand Cherry Pie, 35
Serviceberry Pie, 137
Wild Silk Pie with Cream Cheese
Topping, 161
Pillow Cookies with Hackberry Filling, 84
Pin cherries, *see:* Wild cherries
Plums, 112-117
Asian-Inspired Plum Sauce, 113
dehydrating, 169
Easy Bear Claws, 20
Fruit-Filled Muffins, 146
Fruit-Striped Cookie Fingers, 119
Ham Slice with Piquant Plum Sauce, 116
making juice or purée, 112
Plum Butter, 115
Plum-Dandy Oatmeal Squares, 114
Plum Filling, 117
plum syrup, 163
Six Recipes Using Wild Fruit Juice or
Syrup, 158–162
Spicy Plum Chutney, 141
Wild Plum Jelly, 115
Pork Chops Glazed with Mountain Ash, 99
Pork Loin Chops with Nannyberry
Barbecue Sauce, 109
Pudding Cake, Gooseberry, 73
Pudding Cake, Serviceberry, 138
Pumpkin Tart with Currant Glaze, 60

Q

Quick breads,
Cranberry Bread, 51
Gooseberry Bread with Crumble
Topping, 72
Sweet Autumn Olive Bread, 7

R

Raspberries, 118-125
  Blackberry-Apple Crisp, 15
  Brambleberry Cream Sauce, 157
  Camper's Delight Breakfast, 122
  Chicken with Wild Raspberry Sauce, 120
  Colorful Fruit Salad, 30
  dehydrating, 169
  Easy Bear Claws, 20
  Fruit-Filled Muffins, 146
  Fruits of the Forest Pie, 156
  Fruit-Striped Cookie Fingers, 119
  Fruit Terrine with Elderberry Gel, 64
  making juice or purée, 118
  Mulberry Ripple Cheesecake, 104
  Raspberry-Balsamic Dressing, 125
  Raspberry Dip, 122
  Raspberry Filling, 121
  Raspberry Jelly, 124
  Raspberry Shortcakes, 123
  raspberry syrup, 163
  Refrigerator Cookies with Dried Berries, 9
  Rice Pudding with Wild Berries, 107
  Rustic Black Raspberry Tart, 124
  Sautéed Fish with Thimbleberries, 153
  Six Recipes Using Wild Fruit Juice or Syrup, 158–162
  Thimbleberry Smoothie, 152
  Wild Berry Vinegar, 13
Red Currant and Blue Cheese Butter, 56
Red Cabbage with Juniper and Bacon, 97
Reducing liquid, 121
Refrigerator Cookies with Autumn Olive "Berries", 9
Relishes,
  Fresh Cranberry Relish, 52
  Highbush Peach Relish, 96
Rice Pudding with Wild Berries, 107
Ripe Gooseberry Jelly, 71
Rose hips, 126-129
  making juice or purée, 126
  Marlin with Rose Hip Glaze, 127
  Rose Hip-Apple Jelly, 128
  Rose Hip Jelly, 127
  Rose Hip Soup, 129
  rose hip syrup, 163
  Rose Hip Tea, 126
  Six Recipes Using Wild Fruit Juice or Syrup, 158–162
Russian olives, 130-132
  Coarse Russian Olive Mustard, 131
  making purée, 130
  Oatmeal Muffins with Russian Olive, 132
Rustic Black Raspberry Tart, 124

S

Salads,
  Chicken Salad with Ground Cherries and Almonds, 80
  Colorful Fruit Salad, 30
  Mixed Greens with Strawberries, Honey Pecans and Blue Cheese, 144
Sand cherries, see: Wild cherries
Sand Cherry Pie, 35
Sauces,
  Asian-Inspired Plum Sauce, 113
  Brambleberry Cream Sauce, 157
  Cherry Barbecue Sauce, 36
  Currant-Basil Sauce, 55
  Nannyberry Barbecue Sauce, 109
  Raspberry-Balsamic Dressing, 125
  Smooth Blackberry Sauce, 12
  Spicy Plum Chutney, 141
  Strawberry-Gooseberry Dessert Sauce, 75
  Sweet and Snappy Ground Cherry Salsa, 83
Sautéed Fish with Thimbleberries, 153
Serviceberries, 133-139
  Blackberry-Apple Crisp, 15
  Blueberry Streusel Muffins, 21
  Cookies with Dried Fruit, Nuts and White Chocolate Chips, 28
  dehydrating, 170
  Easy Bear Claws, 20
  Fruit-Filled Muffins, 146
  Fruits of the Forest Pie, 156
  Fruit-Striped Cookie Fingers, 119
  Individual Currant Cheesecakes, 57
  Microwave Oatmeal with Serviceberries and Nuts, 139
  Refrigerator Cookies with Dried Berries, 9
  Serviceberry and Ricotta Brunch Ring, 135
  Serviceberry and Wild Rice Muffins, 136
  Serviceberry Filling, 136
  Serviceberry or Blueberry Freezer Jam, 134
  Serviceberry Pie, 137
  Serviceberry Pudding Cake, 138
  Thimbleberry Smoothie, 152
Shortcakes, Raspberry, 123
Smoothie, Thimbleberry, 152
Smooth Blackberry Sauce, 12
Smooth sumac, see: Sumac
Smoother Blackberry Jam, 17
Sorbet, Highbush Cranberry, 95
Sorbet, Wild Fruit, 158
Soups,
  Curried Sweet Potato Soup with HBC Garnish, 92
  Rose Hip Soup, 129

Spicebush, northern, 140-141
  Jerk Marinade, 140
  Spicy Plum Chutney, 141
  Tart Mountain Ash Jelly, 101
Spice Cake, Highbush Cranberry, 90
Spicy Gooseberry-Apple Crisp, 74
Spicy Plum Chutney, 141
Staghorn sumac, see: Sumac
Sterilizing canning jars and lids, 171
Strawberries, 142-147
  dehydrating, 170
  Easy Bear Claws, 20
  Fruit-Filled Muffins, 146
  Fruit-Striped Cookie Fingers, 119
  Mixed Greens with Strawberries, Honey Pecans and Blue Cheese, 144
  Raspberry Dip, 122
  Refrigerator Cookies with Dried Berries, 9
  Strawberries and Shortbread, 147
  Strawberry Filling, 145
  Strawberry Freezer Jam, 142-143
  Strawberry-Gooseberry Dessert Sauce, 75
  Thimbleberry Smoothie, 152
  Wild Berry Vinegar, 13
  Wild Blueberry Pancakes, 24
Sumac, 148-151
  Cedar-Planked Salmon with Sumac-Maple Glaze, 150
  Elderberry-Sumac Jelly, 63
  making juice, 148
  sumac-ade, 148
  Sumac Tea, 149
Sweet and Snappy Ground Cherry Salsa, 83
Sweet Autumn Olive Bread, 7
Sweet Mountain Ash Jelly, 98
Sweet Potato Soup, Curried, with HBC Garnish, 92
Sweet rolls,
  Blueberry Spirals with Cardamom, 25
  Easy Bear Claws, 20
Syrup, Wild Berry or Fruit, 163

T

Tart Mountain Ash Jelly, 101
Tea, Rose Hip, 126
Tea, Sumac, 149
Thimbleberries, 152-154
  Brambleberry Cream Sauce, 157
  Easy Bear Claws, 20
  Fruit-Filled Muffins, 146
  Fruits of the Forest Pie, 156
  Fruit-Striped Cookie Fingers, 119
  Sautéed Fish with Thimbleberries, 153
  Thimbleberry Filling, 154
  Thimbleberry Smoothie, 152
Tomato paste, saving leftovers, 36
Turkey Breast with Cranberry Pan Sauce, 48
Turnovers, Blackberry, 12

V

Venison Chops or Steaks Glazed with
Mountain Ash, 99
Venison Roast with Mountain Ash and
Juniper Rub, 100
Vinegar, Wild Berry, 13

W

Wild Berry or Fruit Syrup, 163
Wild Berry Vinegar, 13
Wild Blueberry Pancakes, 24
Wild cherries, 31-37
Cherry Barbecue Sauce, 36
Cherry Wigglers, 33
Easy Cherry Applesauce, 37
Elderberry Meringue Pie, 66
Fruit Terrine with Elderberry Gel, 64

Homemade Cherry Cordial, 34
making juice or purée, 31
Pumpkin Tart with Currant Glaze, 60
Sand Cherry Pie, 35
Six Recipes Using Wild Fruit Juice or
Syrup, 158–162
Spicy Plum Chutney, 141
Wild Cherry Jelly, 33
Wild Cherry-Lemonade Sparkler, 35
wild cherry syrup, 163
Wild Cherry Zabaglione, 32
Wild Fruit Gels (Gumdrops), 159
Wild Fruit Sorbet, 158
Wild Plum Jelly, 115
Wild rice, about, 49
Wild Rice and Serviceberry Muffins, 136
Wild Rice with Cranberries and Nuts, 49

Wild Silk Pie with Cream Cheese Topping,
161
**Wintergreen (creeping) and creeping
snowberry**, 155
Wintergreen Malt, 155
Withe-rod, *see:* Nannyberries, withe-rod
and blackhaws

Z

Zabaglione, Wild Cherry, 32
Zesting citrus fruits, 34

BIBLIOGRAPHY

Brill, Steven. *Identifying and Harvesting Edible and Medicinal Plants in Wild (and Not So Wild) Places.* New York, NY: William Morrow, an imprint of HarperCollins Publishers Inc., 1994.

Derig, Betty B. and Fuller, Margaret C. *Wild Berries of the West.* Missoula, MT: Mountain Press Publishing Company, 2001.

Gibbons, Euell. *Stalking the Wild Asparagus.* New York, NY: David McKay Company, Inc., 1962.

Hibler, Janie. *The Berry Bible.* New York, NY: William Morrow, an imprint of HarperCollins Publishers Inc., 2004.

Lyle, Katie Letcher. *The Wild Berry Book: Romance, Recipes and Remedies.* Minnetonka, MN: NorthWord Press, 1994.

Marrone, Teresa. *Abundantly Wild: Collecting and Cooking Wild Edibles in the Upper Midwest* and *The Seasonal Cabin Cookbook.* Cambridge, MN: Adventure Publications, 2004 and 2001.

Marrone, Teresa. *The Back-Country Kitchen: Camp Cooking for Canoeists, Hikers and Anglers.* Minneapolis, MN: Northern Trails Press, 1996.

Peterson, Lee Allen. *A Field Guide to Edible Wild Plants of Eastern and Central North America.* Boston, MA: Houghton Mifflin Company, 1977.

Thayer, Samuel. *The Forager's Harvest.* Ogema, WI: Forager's Harvest, 2006.

U.S. Department of Agriculture, USDA National Nutrient Database for Standard Reference, Release 21 (http://www.ars.usda.gov/nutrientdata).

Young, Kay. *Wild Seasons: Gathering and Cooking Wild Plants of the Great Plains.* Lincoln, NE: University of Nebraska Press, 1993.

ABOUT THE AUTHOR

Teresa Marrone has been gathering and preparing wild edibles for more than 20 years. She was formerly Managing Editor of a series of outdoors-themed cookbooks and other books, and is the author of *Abundantly Wild: Collecting and Cooking Wild Edibles in the Upper Midwest*, as well as numerous outdoors-related cookbooks. Teresa also writes magazine articles on wild foods and cooking. *Cooking with Wild Berries & Fruits of Minnesota, Wisconsin and Michigan* combines her various skills and interests into a clear, concise, easy-to-use book that helps the user appreciate the diversity of the various wild berries and fruits that grow in this region. Teresa lives in Minneapolis with husband Bruce and their Senegal parrot, Tuca.